Praise for
Imperfect Courage

"Jessica's perspective of global sisterhood and the power of lifting one another up in the midst of fear and scarcity is exactly what we need today. This book is both an invitation and a challenge to bravely show up for ourselves, for the people we love, and for the strangers we will one day call family. I say, 'Amen!'"

—BRENÉ BROWN, PHD, #1 *New York Times* best-selling author
of *Braving the Wilderness*

"I absolutely love this book. Jessica is smart, brave, honest, and funny, and this book is the perfect mix of listening-ear and kick-in-the-pants. Equal parts compassion and challenge, this is a must-read for all of us who want to make a difference with our lives but sometimes find fear and anxiety standing in the way."

—SHAUNA NIEQUIST, *New York Times* best-selling author
of *Present Over Perfect* and *Bread and Wine*

"Sometimes a desperate need creates an opportunity to transform the world. Jessica's story provides a beautifully imperfect tapestry for understanding what surrender and courage can look like when unexpected need tests our faith. She shows us that stepping into our stories can build a path to change someone else's story. Learn how to harness your fear and transform it into courage that will change the world."

—LATASHA MORRISON, founder and president of Be the Bridge

"Pick your reason to read this book: you care about the world, you are an entrepreneur, you love fashion, you love women, you have big ideas, you have a global mind-set, you are a builder, a dreamer, a visionary, a Texan (there is plenty of Texas in Jessica's story). *Imperfect Courage* is fuel for all of these. It is as generous and adventurous as Jessica, who is the greatest leader, creator, and friend I've ever known."

—JEN HATMAKER, *New York Times* best-selling author of
Of Mess and Moxie and host of the *For the Love* podcast

"Jessica Honegger has written a must-read account of how the work of justice goes hand in hand with women's empowerment. And it all starts with steps of imperfect courage."

—MELISSA RUSSELL, chief advancement officer
for International Justice Mission

"Jessica is such an incredible example of what a leader in business should be. Not only because she's had the courage to push herself to create a company from the ground up, but because she made her way down the road to success and then turned around and held a lantern up to light the way for the rest of us. This is a must-read for anyone who's chasing big dreams on a road that feels unsteady!"

—RACHEL HOLLIS, *New York Times* best-selling author
of *Girl, Wash Your Face*

"As the CEO of Noonday Collection, Jessica—with her lack of pretense and commitment to transparency—has earned the trust of artisans and consumers alike. She brings that same approach to *Imperfect Courage;* each chapter feels like a personal invitation to ride alongside Jessica as she recounts memories that tell of her infectious passion for using entrepreneurship to empower women all over the globe. Her deep conviction for equality and justice is contagious and will change the lives of so many."

—MICA MAY, founder and CEO of May Designs

"Jessica Honegger will captivate you with her adventure of building a company that is shaping and changing the world. You will find yourself crying, laughing, and wondering why you've played it so safe in life. She makes you want to risk it all for the good of people and the world, because doing so doesn't just make life more meaningful; it makes it more fun!"

—JENNIE ALLEN, author of *Nothing to Prove* and founder
and visionary of IF:Gathering

"Jessica inspires me to think so much bigger than my own two hands. I'm so moved by her heart and tenacity as an entrepreneur and by her commitment to connecting, empowering, and motivating women around the world!"

—EMILY LEY, founder of Simplified and best-selling author
of *Grace, Not Perfection* and *A Simplified Life*

"This book is your road map to uncovering and pursuing your big dream. Jessica teaches us all how to get past the lies that keep us from living our full potential in the world. As *Imperfect Courage* illustrates, the more each of us broadens our circle of compassion and embraces the entire globe, the faster the love of God makes it to every corner of the world."

—AMY BROWN, co-host of *The Bobby Bones Show*

"In this lovely book, Jessica opens up about the rocky journey of starting Noonday Collection, what she has learned along the way, and how she's better because of the people she's met. I'm so excited for you to read this story not just so you'll know more about Jessica and Noonday but so you'll know more about yourself and how you, too, can do big things—even if you are scared."

—JAMIE IVEY, author of *If You Only Knew* and host
of *The Happy Hour with Jamie Ivey* podcast

"Jessica Honegger's journey is an inspiration not just to entrepreneurs and business leaders but to anyone seeking to pursue the dreams God puts in their hearts. *Imperfect Courage* is living proof that fashion can play an important part in changing the world and business can be an incredible force for good. The world needs more businesses like Noonday Collection and more mindfully ambitious leaders like Jessica Honegger."

—MEGAN TAMTE, founder and co-CEO of Evereve

LIVE A LIFE OF PURPOSE BY LEAVING
COMFORT AND GOING SCARED

IMPERFECT COURAGE

JESSICA HONEGGER
FOUNDER AND CO-CEO OF NOONDAY COLLECTION

WATERBROOK

IMPERFECT COURAGE

All Scripture quotations are taken from the Holy Bible, New International Version®, NIV®. Copyright © 1973, 1978, 1984, 2011 by Biblica Inc.® Used by permission. All rights reserved worldwide.

Details in some anecdotes and stories have been changed to protect the identities of the persons involved. Details have been recalled to the best of the author's memory.

Hardcover ISBN 978-0-7352-9129-4
eBook ISBN 978-0-7352-9130-0

Copyright © 2018 by Jessica Honegger

Cover design by Joy Gallagher

Published in the United States by WaterBrook, an imprint of the Crown Publishing Group, a division of Penguin Random House LLC, New York.

WATERBROOK® and its deer colophon are registered trademarks of Penguin Random House LLC.

Library of Congress Cataloging-in-Publication Data
Names: Honegger, Jessica, author.
Title: Imperfect courage : live a life of purpose by leaving comfort and going scared / Jessica Honegger, founder & co-CEO, Noonday Collection.
Description: First Edition. | Colorado Springs : WaterBrook, 2018. | Includes bibliographical references.
Identifiers: LCCN 2017058595| ISBN 9780735291294 (hardcover) | ISBN 9780735291300 (electronic)
Subjects: LCSH: Honegger, Jessica. | Businesswomen—Religious life. | Businesswomen—Biography. | Entrepreneurship—Religious aspects—Christianity. | Business—Religious aspects—Christianity. | Christian biography.
Classification: LCC BV4596.B8 H66 2018 | DDC 248.4—dc23
LC record available at https://lccn.loc.gov/2017058595

Printed in the United States of America
2018—First Edition

10 9 8 7 6 5 4 3 2 1

For Joe,
who made me a promise
once that changed the world.

CONTENTS

The path to success is straight, and the experience of walking it is marked by both confidence and clarity.

No One, ever

INTRODUCTION

GIVE IT A GO

CASH IS KING WHEN YOU OWN A BUSINESS," my entrepreneurial dad has always liked to say, and here I was standing at the counter of an Austin pawnshop living out this truth. After visiting several different pawnshops, I settled on the most promising one, clutching a fistful of precious gold jewelry that my mom and grandmother had given me over the years—my confirmation cross, my sixteenth birthday ring, my middle school graduation necklace—and prepared myself to sell off all of it to keep my dream of my homegrown business, Noonday Collection, alive. This scene hardly meshed with the posh and privileged debutante parties of my youth, but desperate times call for desperate measures. I was pawnshop desperate, it seemed.

Based on the conversation that was unfolding between the man behind the counter and me, I knew that I was being had. But this is how things go when you're needy and rushed: you impulsively take the first semireasonable offer that comes along. "You've got a deal," I told the guy. "Nine hundred for it all."

I left the pawnshop feeling victorious, even as doubts scratched at the back of my mind. Would I later regret this decision to forever part with my family heirlooms? The Noonday website had been a rudimentary one at best, and I knew that I needed to invest more than the paltry fee that my friend Joel had benevolently charged me to get a more robust website off the ground. I needed a *real* site, and in line with the adage "It takes money to make money," I needed this cash to grow—to make my business *real*.

A spirit of entrepreneurship has flowed through my veins since I was old enough to hawk my handmade bandana banana clips for a profit, and even though I was terrified to step into the unknown, I was a woman on a mission—to build a business and to bring home a bright-eyed little boy named Jack.

Prior to launching Noonday in 2010, my husband, Joe, and I were parents to two—a girl, Amelie, and a boy, Holden—but were considering growing our family through adoption.

We had met and fallen in love years prior during a training program with Food for the Hungry, a relief and development organization serving the world's most vulnerable people. We soon realized that the thing that made our two hearts beat fast was partnering with those who were living in material poverty, often where injustice was great. One year after we'd met, Joe proposed to me on a wobbly pier over Lake Atitlán in Guatemala,[1] where we lived at the time.

I've since returned to this beautiful town several times to visit artisan partners there, and every time I can't help but think back on those early married-life days, when we were just starting to dream about how we could build a life of impact together.

Joe and I settled into life after getting married, always with the intention of living internationally again. But then our two littles arrived, as did our Austin house-flipping business. We would purchase, remodel, redecorate, and list every residence we could, and while we enjoyed the entrepreneurial challenge of real estate, we still held those Food for the Hungry days close to our hearts. On many occasions, we would look at each other following yet another tile-versus-concrete argument and shake our heads. Was a life of purpose reserved for idealistic singles in their twenties? Or was it meant for home flippers with a growing family too?

Joe and I took many international trips to visit friends and not-for-profits to continue to learn about sustainable solutions toward poverty alleviation. These trips also served to keep our perception of the illusionary American Dream in check—and to remind us that life for most of the world looked very different. On one of those trips, I held a child orphaned by the HIV crisis in my arms for the first time since becoming a mother myself. It was then that I felt a stirring in my heart that told me we would eventually grow our family through adoption.

After Joe and I discussed the possibility of adopting internationally and realized that our hearts were aligned, we began to prepare ourselves for what this next big step could look like for us. It was during this season of preparation that we booked a trip to Uganda to visit friends. One of the couples we visited on that trip was Bobby and Downie Mickler, who had relocated from Texas to Uganda, with hopes of creating entrepreneurial opportunities for people living there in need of work. With Texas pecans in hand, we paid them a visit and brought them a taste from home.

One Sunday afternoon, Joe and I sat on their porch as Bobby explained how his work was going. Some of the businesses he'd helped launch were small—the man who started a full-on plumbing business from his bicycle, for example—while others were big, such as the creation of an innovative mosquito-repellant spray system that larger hotels in the area were putting to use. As Bobby went on about one of the businesses he cared for most, his passion rose. "We have friends here who are *incredible* artists," he said. "Their names are Jalia and Daniel Matovu. We sent several crates of their goods back home and tried to create a marketplace for them on our visits. But we have realized that this endeavor needs a lot more attention if it's really going to succeed. Downie's mom has two crates left—bags, scarves, jewelry pieces, that sort of thing. Would you be interested in selling them?"

Downie went on to fill me in on Jalia and Daniel, explaining that the sale of their handmade goods was the only thing keeping them afloat week by week. "They are committed to using their art to provide for themselves and their kids and eventually, they hope, their extended family and friends," Downie said. "I believe that they are the future of Uganda, but right now they barely get food on the table . . ."

I listened intently, nodding as the story of this tenacious but struggling couple sparked something deep in my heart. Since my time with Food for the Hungry, I was convinced that a good job was the surest and most dignified way to empower a family to rise out of poverty. These people, Jalia and Daniel, sounded like my people. I tucked that knowledge away, not really believing that I'd ever play a part in their story.

————————

Joe and I arrived home from that trip refreshed, filled with vision and eager to adopt. We weren't sure that Uganda was where we'd find our child, but we still felt confident that international adoption was the path for us. Our small nest egg would provide the means; now it was time to research the way.

What we didn't foresee (but perhaps should have) was that the next month the Austin real estate bubble would pop with the advent of the recession. That adoption nest egg we boasted in? Yeah, it started paying the grocery bill. At its worst, Joe and I owned five houses, one of which we were living in and four of which we needed to sell. Three of them showed no signs of selling—stressful, to say the least. Joe and I began playing chess with our credit cards, and still today, I remember the look on my husband's face each time he came into our bedroom on errand day. In a quiet voice, he'd say, "Use the Mastercard today, not the Visa, okay?"

It was a hard season for us—both financially and otherwise. During sleepless nights, I stayed awake wondering if the four of us were going to have to move in with my parents. However, with the current real estate reality, our house would never sell, so round and round it all went in my head. One day, I received a call from Joe on his way home from what was supposed to have been a closed real estate deal—the only one in months.

"She backed out," he said. "The client was too worried the home was going to depreciate in value."

The despair led me to googling, "What to do when God has led you toward international adoption but you have no money." Nothing helpful popped up.

Okay, so maybe I never googled that exactly, but I did begin to pluck my way through the internet, determined to find direction of some sort. Within a month of beginning that process, two things happened that I could only explain as divine nudges. The first was an email I received from a friend who had just returned from Rwanda after interviewing for a job with International Justice Mission. "I heard through the grapevine that you are exploring adoption," he wrote. He went on to say that he had met a woman on his trip, Jennifer, who lived in

Rwanda. She had recently finalized the adoption of her son and wanted to begin facilitating adoptions for American families.

The second nudge felt even more exacting. I searched online for additional information regarding adopting from Rwanda, and one of the first hits I got was a blog by a fellow Austinite who was months away from adopting a little boy from Rwanda. Intrigued by her story, I reached out to her through her site to see if she could offer us any words of wisdom. "We should meet up," she responded. As I set the date in my calendar, I decided to take a closer look at her blog, and as I scanned her About Me page, I noticed her maiden name and saw her photo. My jaw dropped. This woman was no stranger; she'd been my college roommate. The nudge became more of a push. "Maybe *Rwanda* is it," I said to Joe.

By this point I knew that to fund our adoption expenses, Joe and I would need to ask for money from family and friends (a prospect that mortified me) or I would need to start a side hustle of some sort. I reached out to Downie in Uganda via text.

"I'm interested in selling those goods after all," I told her, and soon enough, I was road-tripping to San Antonio to pick up those crates of vibrant, beaded Ugandan goods while reaching out to all the Austin-based friends I knew to invite them to my first trunk show. There I would sell Jalia and Daniel's handmade goods, many clothes from my own closet, and spare sets of my dishes, in hopes of getting one step closer to my adoption fund-raising goal.

The day leading up to the party, I felt junior-high-like fear rising to meet me. I was suddenly gripped by the conviction that this was all a big mistake. I was convinced no one would come, and then I wondered what people would think if they did. The guest room was filled to the brim with clothes, my grandma's dishes lined the fireplace, and rows of paper beads were laid out on the dining table. What if pursuing this dream was a fool's errand? I almost canceled then and there, as fear of rejection and failure stared me in the face. But instead, I sat in my living room and gathered my courage, imperfect though it was. I decided to simply go scared.

Little did I know then that that night I would be launching what would become the largest fair-trade jewelry company in the world. And that in only five years, Noonday Collection would be named by *Inc. Magazine* as the forty-fifth fastest growing business in the United States. Or that, two years after that, I would stand on a stage next to my now business partner, Travis Wilson, to accept the Ernst & Young Entrepreneur of the Year award—an honor shared by Whole Foods' John Mackey, among others.

My fears may have come out in droves that night, but thankfully, my friends did too. As did those friends' friends, whom they'd invited. They came because they *did* care about our new journey toward international adoption, and once in my home surrounded by all the African goods, they were utterly compelled—by the intersections of fashion and impact, style and story, work and dignity, and profit and purpose. An hour into the party, I was shocked to find that I had sold more than 90 percent of all that I had.

As the last of my guests left with their purchases, I wondered if there wasn't something to this concept. After that night, I started dreaming bigger than I'd dreamed before. The products were distinctive, the backstory was compelling, the gap in the market was evident, and the power of women gathering together for each other, face to face, was real. In fact, Noonday exists because women showed up for me on that humble evening in our home. Emboldened by such support, I decided to see where this path would lead.

That first trunk show led to another, and to another after that. I had no business cards at those early events, so I'd scribble down my name and number on yellow sticky notes, handing them out to anyone who expressed interest in hosting her own trunk show.

As money trickled in—fifteen dollars for a bracelet, thirty dollars for a necklace, twenty dollars for a scarf, all of it cash only—I'd reach out directly to Jalia and Daniel via email in Uganda to order more. Joe and I scrambled to set up a Western Union account to wire money to them while Jalia and Daniel scrambled to figure out how to order raw materials, price their items, and sell them to me. After each show I would order fresh stock of exactly what I'd just sold and get busy booking my next trunk show, where I'd do it all over again. It was a pretty stripped-down process, but what I lacked in infrastructure, I made up for in drive.

Across these last seven years, my "little jewelry thing" has bloomed into a thriving global direct-sales brand that has employed more than four thousand Noonday business owners in the United States and over forty-five hundred artisan partners in twelve countries around the world. Jalia and Daniel, who formerly lived on less than two dollars per day, are now part of Uganda's middle class and employ more than three hundred local people, many of whom are single moms. Closer to home, our son Jack's adoption has been completed and he is now an official part of our family. At eight years old, that thoughtful and energetic boy is a daily reminder to me of the value of courage—and of choosing to say yes to big dreams, even when fear is knocking at the door.

Until I started this Noonday journey, I had always equated *courage* to the word *fearlessness*. In my mind, courage described people such as Martin Luther King Jr., who rallied a crowd every time he spoke, despite the danger that rally inevitably drew; firefighters who ran into the

Twin Towers on 9/11, while everyone else was running out; women who leave their abusive spouses, having no idea what will happen next. *That*, I told myself, was courage. On the day we moved forward with the adoption process despite what our bank account said or the night I opened up my home for possibly no one to come or the day I pawned my gold jewelry, I had not felt like a hero. And yet, with a beating heart and shaking hands, I said yes to risk and yes to moving ahead. I had simply gone scared.

Imperfect courage is the only kind I possessed, but it was courage nonetheless. Instead of waiting for fear to subside, I had made it my friend. Because when you've got a vision, you don't have time to wait around for your fears to vanish before you start moving. Perhaps the hero's journey is not for a few brave people after all but is an invitation to me, to us all, to rally our courage and go do the thing we're meant to do. This mind-blowing transformation—from letting fear sideline you to choosing to go scared—is what I wish for you. And so, my friend, this book: a memoir-ish road map to get us from here to there.

We're going to do this thing in three parts, because all the best things come in threes: Corona, salt, lime; morning, noon, night; location, location, location. In part 1, we will accomplish a little inner reckoning, that painful but fundamental work that invites courage into our lives from the inside out. What are you afraid of, and what toll is that fear taking in your life? I'm not here to tell you to stop feeling afraid; instead, this book is a guide to *going scared*. To not waiting around for your nerves and your nerve to reconcile. Still, if we're going to *go*, we've got to understand the things that are holding us back.

In part 2, we'll explore the wonders of togetherness as well as the dangers of going it alone in our quest for living a life that counts, both for ourselves and for a world in need. If you're a lone ranger type, then you'll hate part 2, but listen to me: you may not skip it. It holds the key that will unlock your fear and empower you to move ahead.

And then in part 3, I bring out my coach's whistle, waking you up, getting you in the game, insisting (but in a lovably encouraging way) that you *bring everything you've got* to this one life that you have been given, to make a meaningful impact for others.

That thing that makes you come alive that you've just been waiting for the courage to do? It's time to give it a go.

PART ONE

THE FIRST STEP

ONE

CHOOSE COURAGE

Courage is being scared to death
but saddling up anyway.

John Wayne

I'T'S THE SUMMER OF 2017, AND OUR GROUP has just arrived in Uganda, returning to the place where Noonday Collection all began. I hear the drums beating in the distance, and my heartbeat falls into rhythm with the percussionists' tempo. Our group has come from all over the United States; social entrepreneurs—at Noonday, we call them ambassadors—who have achieved some serious sales goals to arrive at this moment and finally put faces to the names of the artisans they've known only from photographs. The surreal nature of the moment hits me as we step out of the van onto the red dirt road that leads to the jewelry workshop. It's a journey that seven years ago I couldn't have imagined, as I sat hunkered in my guest bedroom with nothing but a handful of paper-bead necklaces.

I sneak behind the gate before the rest of my group and I are met with a tidal wave of tight hugs, swishing skirts, and joyful laughter. As the ambassadors emerge and are swept up in this celebratory parade, I tell them to resist the urge to get out their phones and snap photos. "Just be present!" I insist, raising my voice above the music. I don't want us to miss a nanosecond of this experience.

As I scan the familiar faces of my artisan friends—Mama Sham with her impossibly bright grin, Bukenya with a trace of a joke always on his face, Latifa with her eager smile, Caleb with his sturdy hand-shake, Rosetta with her freshly cut hair, Mama Jabal with her ever-changing head covering, and Nakato with her shy countenance—I think of the long journey we've all been on together. Seven years ago, I couldn't imagine starting a business that fostered a global sisterhood. My little jewelry business has become more than I ever dreamed it could be.

After the first trunk show, things really took off—women showed in-creased interest, I had multiple trunk shows after that, and the business emerged as one that was *real*. After a few months' work, demand grew not just in Austin but in cities across the country. I began to dream of what it would be like to work this business with other impact-hungry people like me. If I could multiply myself, then jobs across the world would multiply too, I figured; I was determined to see if I was right. But before I had a chance to start recruiting, I received an email from a woman in Seattle who had gotten wind of Noonday via another mom's adoption blog. She wrote,

> My name is Sara. I would be interested in hosting a Noonday trunk show, but I'm also wondering if it would be possible to do more than that. I'm interested in working with your company to host Noonday trunk shows in the Seattle area—to earn income

toward my family's own adoption, to help others raise funds, and to make a difference in the lives of women in Uganda and around the world. Like you, I've had the opportunity to travel and to volunteer in places such as Argentina, Guatemala, and Pakistan. I'm passionate about the not-just-for-profit business model and would be excited to work with your company. Would you be interested in talking more about what that could look like?

Why, yes, I would . . .

Sara and I began to exchange emails, exploring a compensation model for this impromptu arrangement, and within a couple of months, Sara became the first Noonday Collection ambassador and held the first-ever Noonday trunk show outside of Texas.

My vision was beginning to spread, and soon, more women were saying yes to launching their own Noonday businesses. Without realizing it, they had become Noonday's first official ambassadors. In the next seven years, Noonday Collection would grow to add artisan partners in Guatemala, Ethiopia, Kenya, Rwanda, Ecuador, Peru, India, Vietnam, Nepal, Afghanistan, and more; we would add ambassadors in every state across America; and we would sell nearly two million accessories, ship more than six hundred thousand orders, and raise more than half a million dollars for adoptive families through the adoption fund-raiser trunk shows we continue to hold to this day.

In Uganda, as I watch my artisan friends dance, I reflect on how hopeful Jalia and I were seven years prior regarding the possibilities for this little endeavor, yet I was aware then that we each had taken wild risks to make it happen. Although the idea had gained traction, to be sure, most of the time I felt utterly incapable of leading the way. While I was passionate about my business's success, I still had so much fear. I wondered about the outcome, whether that be failure or success, and I lay awake many nights worrying about both. Failure would mean lost livelihoods and perhaps a waste of all this time and effort. Success would mean more responsibility and a dramatic shift in how I spent my time—less Play-Doh and more PowerPoint. Was I really qualified to run a global business? My résumé said an emphatic no. Was I able to be an attentive and caring mom while also leading the company?

During that time of uncertainty, on the other side of the world, Jalia, too, had taken a leap of faith in our partnership by hiring her first employees, all people who were living in acute poverty and for whom I felt the high stakes of their success. It was painfully clear to me that if I failed in this endeavor, there was more at stake than just my personal success. In moments of despair, that singular thought kept me from caving in. It fueled my earnest belief, and it bolstered my determination that nothing was going to keep me from building this thing I was building—not financial desperation, not mom-of-two-kids-under-three (so far) exhaustion, not direct-sales cynicism, not unfavorable odds of *any* kind. If I was going to make it, I couldn't wait around for my fears to dismiss themselves. Courage cornered me, and I accepted its challenge, regardless of what the cost would be.

One of my favorite thinkers and mentors, Andy Crouch, has a saying that my family has adopted for ourselves, which is that "the only thing money can buy is bubble wrap."[1] Andy's sentiment is aimed primarily at North Americans who, by being born here, are among the most affluent in the world. Affluence and privilege can be used for incredible good—and I hope that by the end of this book you will awaken to the power your privilege can wield—but it can also insulate us from the best (and worst) things that life may bring our way. I know that being born in a wealthy zip code to two white, resourced parents certainly insulated me from the realities of racism, poverty, and injustices that many people around the world face daily. Truly, no matter how broke Joe and I may have felt during our real estate demise and adoption journey, we were not selling our prized-possession leather-bound Bible to get money for the only meal our family would have that week, which is what Jalia and Daniel once had to do.

I've always been passionate about *going* in life—going out of my comfort zone, going straight through my fears, *going scared*. And yet even I acknowledge that there are myriad benefits to staying put: comfort, safety, and plush couches, to name a few.

Take Netflix, for example. Is there anything more satisfying than tucking yourself into a comfy couch, remote in one hand, smartphone in the other, binge-watching *Friday Night Lights* and scrolling through your social media feeds? Comfort. Safety. Security. Alrightness. Call it the siren song of the recliner. When we are seated, we cannot fall. Am I right? My own children, accident prone though they may be, have never broken an arm while watching TV.

It's tempting to bubble-wrap our lives. Layer upon layer of protection means we stay unbroken, right through to the end. We wrap ourselves in fear. We wrap ourselves in isolation. We wrap ourselves in nightly glasses of wine or in our beloved Instagram feed. We avoid real issues involving real people who live in the real world because, *What if*

I get hurt? And yet what does this approach yield for us? A life of boredom, a lack of impact, spiritual death.

"Amidst safety the world has never before known," Andy wrote, "the greatest spiritual struggle many of us face is to be willing to take off our bubble wrap."[2]

We know that outside our front door, something much more fulfilling lies in wait. But instead of pursing the desires of our heart, we spend our energy in defense mode, trying to avoid disappointment, betrayal, and pain. Something in us clings to these places of safety and makes it difficult to stand—even as something deeper within us longs to stand up, to eventually rise.

Here on the couch, you and me, we can't make a misstep. We can't break a limb here. We can't get shamed here.

And yet. (Here is where I may gently tug that cozy blanket off you.) We know down in the marrow of our bones that we were made for something more.

———

My original motivation for writing this book hinged on a single thought: There is a whole world out there begging for us to use the opportunity we have been given, to create opportunity for others, so that we—*all of us*—can flourish. So, while comfort may beckon us, choosing courage will always be the route to impact.

When we first step out of our comfort zones to embrace our larger world, a small but meaningful revolution takes place inside us as formerly invisible injustices are juxtaposed against a bubble-wrapped reality. Even now, when I think back to the day when my teenage eyes were first opened to the harsh realities faced by so many people in our world,

I can feel the weight of it hitting me afresh, like being plunged into ice-cold water after spending my whole life comfortably warm.

When I was fifteen years old, I signed up to volunteer on a trip to Kenya with my church. There in East Africa, I would witness the obstacles faced by many people living in poverty and see with fresh perspective just how many resources I had at my disposal. Where I grew up, many kids received new cars on their sixteenth birthday, friends spent their weekends four-wheeling around ranches that had been passed down through generations of Texans, and life revolved around the Fiesta social events of San Antonio. It was a far cry from what I would see in Kenya. My world was about to get rocked.

When my church group landed in Nairobi, I took in the bustling city. Amid the dizzying scene, the image of one woman stood out to me, the contrast of her bright eyes impossible to miss. Set against a backdrop of dusty shanties and corrugated-metal-roofed lean-tos, one crawling on top of the next as far as the eye could see, was a makeshift set of wooden shelves, held erect by sawed-off tree limbs that supported a well-worn tarp. Positioned precariously but with great intention on those shelves were baskets of fruits and vegetables—tomatoes and bananas, avocados and mangos, potatoes and cabbages—their vibrant hues catching my eye.

One of my Kenyan friends explained that this woman was a new entrepreneur, her bustling stand made possible by a microcredit loan she had recently received. Evidently, the woman's husband, an abusive man who drank any earnings he brought home from odd jobs, was not providing for his children. So she had decided to take matters into her own hands. I was immediately inspired by this woman's spirit. Though our lives and motivations were very different, I, too, had an entrepreneurial itch. From the jewelry stands I set up as a kid where I would hawk my handmade banana clips and conch earrings to the no-frills day camp I launched in junior high for grade-schoolers in my neighborhood, I had always been attracted to the idea of multiplying whatever resources I had into something much more. And this woman was taking what she had been given and *running with it,* transforming simple fruits and vegetables into economic empowerment.

My fifteen-year-old self would have been incredulous had I been told that one day I'd return to those very same streets as an adult, offering up entrepreneurial opportunities for other Kenyans living in the slums. The fact that Noonday now partners with eighty-five talented metalworkers in Nairobi is one of the sweetest serendipities I've known in life. And it's a beautiful reminder that you and I can take the resources we've been given and invest them for good in this world. Yes, such investments will cost us something—comfort, security, control. But impact doesn't come from the couch dweller, right? It comes from those with imperfect courage who choose to go scared. In the same way that a toddler learns to walk by walking, we get our *courage* legs under us only when we stand to our feet and *move.*

TWO

STAND UP

Sometimes the place you are used
to is not the place you belong.

Katende, in *Queen of Katwe*

DESPITE A DWINDLING BANK ACCOUNT and several unsold houses
on the market, Joe and I launched headlong into international
adoption. We knew what the outcome would be—our third child. We
just didn't know how we would fund that turn of events. This is what
faith is about, I suppose, and exercising it was both exhilarating and
terrifying to us.

In the end, cash did appear, in the form of Noonday revenue and
generous checks from friends who longed to support our adoption efforts, and now we found ourselves in Rwanda, ready to finalize our
adoption of Jack. Whatever concerns we'd carried regarding finances or
logistics were dwarfed by the one remaining piece to our family-growth
puzzle: getting an official ruling from an in-country judge. Of course,
we weren't the only couple desiring such a declaration; on the morning
when we reported to the judge's modest chambers, we were herded into
the hot, dimly lighted office with six other families, our stomachs churn-
ing, all of us fearing delays.

The sense of dread that accompanied us had trailed us the entire way. One year prior, I received an email from Jennifer, my adoption liaison-turned-friend, that said, "Jessica, I don't have all the details yet, but you will need to expedite your Rwandan paperwork . . . now."

Evidently, Rwanda's Official People in Charge had made the decision to refuse any new adoption applications, and so all applications that were not received within forty-eight hours' time would be declined. When those two days had come and gone, the new ruling would take effect, and families who hadn't been able to pivot quickly enough would be left holding nothing but their inch-thick application booklet (what fellow adoptive parents know as a *dossier*) and unrealized hope. Even worse, the children waiting for families would have to keep waiting.

"We have to get to the officials in Austin, and next to [then secretary of state Hillary] Clinton's office in DC," I frantically explained to Joe, when he asked what expediting would entail. We needed signatures—lots of signatures—acknowledging this, authenticating that, approving our application in full, but based on what we were hearing from those in the know, our chances were slim.

"DC is refusing paperwork too," Jennifer told us. "They're overwhelmed just like everybody. I'm not sure they'll accept your dossier, even if you deliver it by hand." At that news, hot tears coursed along my cheeks. Joe and I had invested so much already: prayers and time and money and heart . . . Was this how it all would end?

Joe is as steady as they come, never rash, rarely impulsive, pretty much always levelheaded, especially when the stakes are high. He looked at me with resolve in his eyes and said, "Then DC is where we'll go. I've got things here covered, babe." And with that came a surge of hope.

Within the hour, I had ushered our two littles into the car and raced to downtown Austin to secure proper signatures on dotted lines, while Joe purchased a last-minute ticket to DC so that I could beg autographs from officials there too. The adrenaline surged as I raced through this day and kept my fears at bay. But as I finally stepped on the plane to DC, fear rose to stare me straight in the face.

I had not hailed a taxi alone in years, and so I called an old friend to see if she could give me a ride from the airport. I was afraid of a cab ride alone. I stepped onto DC's metro and was sure I would never find the right stop. A woman standing next to me noticed my anxiety and asked how she could help. She ended up walking me to the right governmental offices. When I arrived, I just knew I had missed hearing my number called. Fear always seems to show up at the most inopportune times. *Just focus on the next thing you must do,* I told myself. *One foot in front of the other; one step at a time. Keep standing. Keep moving. Keep going, Jessica . . . Keep going scared.*

I finally arrived at the Rwandan embassy, armed with a few Kinyarwanda phrases and baked goods from the shop around the corner (because if you're going to ask someone for a favor, doughnuts never hurt). Several other families were there, fellow hopefuls who had also hopped on airplanes to get their paperwork pushed through. I engaged many of them in conversation, hearing their stories, wishing them well, but truly, my attention was fixed on one thing: Would Joe and I ever be able to adopt?

After an entire day spent camping out in the embassy, the embassy workers told me that they had stamped our paperwork and that, miracle of miracles, it would shortly be on its way to Rwanda. I breathed the deepest sigh of relief as I dished out thank-yous to everyone I saw and headed for home. I pushed past my fears, and the first hurdle was over.

Little did I know that the complications involved in international adoption had only begun.

———————

Fourteen months later, Joe and I received the long-awaited call from Jennifer. "Are you guys in front of a computer?" she asked. "I have someone to introduce you to." We called out to our two littles and told them it was time to meet their brother. Joe clicked on the attachment Jennifer had sent our way, and there was our little boy. Almond-shaped eyes. Luscious little lips. They had given him the name Jacques, and eventually we'd call him Jack, a family name that his great-grandfather already shared. Jack Honegger . . . Soon he'd be ours.

Two weeks after that call, I boarded my scheduled flight to Rwanda for the final step in the process—legally making Jack our son. At this point, most of what I knew of Rwanda had come via the 2004 movie *Hotel Rwanda* and a stack of books I had read, but when the plane touched down in the land of a thousand hills, my heart felt at home.

Jennifer awaited my arrival, along with Joe, who had flown ahead, and Norbert, the Rwandan attorney we had hired. Upon receiving my boisterous hug, he offered me tender kisses on each of my cheeks. For the better part of two hours, Joe and I sat in a stuffy government office, signing our lives away, it seemed. And then we headed for the orphanage. At last, it was time to meet our boy.

Fear came flooding back on the night before Jack and I met. *Would this child want me? Would I be stripping him from his culture and people? Would I feel love? Would he feel love?*

Joe and I stood in the orphanage courtyard with sweaty palms and racing hearts. The head mother of Missionaries of Charity told us that

Jacques was on his way. I caught sight of a woman in a nun's habit making her way toward us, a beautiful two-and-a-half-year-old toddler in hand. "Is that him?" I asked, not wanting to approach the wrong child. After all, there were other waiting families. But that little boy—indeed, he was our Jack.

I reached out my arms to him, and as he allowed me to scoop him up, I thought my heart might burst. All the hoping, praying, surrendering, hustling, longing, sleepless nights . . . the waiting of it all . . . the wonder of it all, and now here was this child in my arms. Mother and son, born not of body but of soul. It was awkward, and it was wonderful. It was full of instant connection and hesitant curiosity, of certainty and doubt. There is something uniquely miraculous about that first meeting between mama and a child birthed through adoption. I was experiencing a miracle that day.

Jack shied away from Joe, signaling that maybe he wasn't yet ready for a man's embrace. Joe simply placed his hand on Jack's back, and then Joe and I cried, and prayed, and were filled to overflowing with gratitude and joy.

The following morning, on our first day together outside the orphanage, we visited a local restaurant where Jack proceeded to eat a man-sized portion of eggs. Clueless that his eyes were bigger than his appetite, we just let him dive in. After the meal, as I hoisted him into the carrier on my back, the little guy lost his too-big-for-his-tummy lunch. With barf in my hair and dribbling down my back, I officially felt like *Jack's mom.* He was mine now, and all that awaited us before we could let him spend the night outside the orphanage was an official proclamation from a judge.

The next day, Norbert met us, wearing the traditional black lawyer's robe required for an appearance in court.

As the judge entered the room and with an expressionless gaze assumed his seat behind the desk, I cut my eyes to the left and to the right, desperate to know what the other families thought, those who were here for the same reason we were. Would this judge find Joe and me worthy to parent a child who bore his likeness, his language, and his culture? The judge was upward of seven feet tall. This is not reinterpreted memory, I'm telling you; I have photographic proof.

Our ragtag collection took him in, as silence washed over us like a wave. Several hushed moments passed as I considered what to do. Someone needed to speak up, but who? Butterflies flittered around my insides as I reflected on every Rwanda-related Google search I had done prior to leaving the States. The one I hadn't thought to enter: "Rwandan Judicial Protocol." Was it appropriate for me, a foreigner—and a foreign *woman,* at that—to stand up, to speak up, to take things into my own hands? Or was the proper response simply to wait quietly, not rocking the boat (especially when that boat belonged to one so intimidating and tall)? The stakes were so high that I couldn't afford a misstep here. I needed courage, and I needed it *now.*

I had stood at this crossroads dozens of times before, my big Texas mouth narrowly silenced by my polite southern-girl heart. My mom had given me the nickname of *lo mismo,* which means "same" in Spanish, in honor of how similar I was to my father, a gregarious fireball of a human being. An entrepreneur always up for adventure, I figured my footsteps would follow in his. At the same time, my mom was the nurturing peacekeeper in our home, and isn't a little girl supposed to lean into her mother's lead?

Where I grew up, that was certainly the expectation. For me that should have meant graduating from high school, joining a sorority, and returning home for debutante season where I would attend weekly parties to try to find a husband, whose career I would then fervently support.

When talking this subject over with my mom for the purposes of writing this book, she smiled knowingly and asked if I remembered how just prior to my dad's arrival home from work each day, she would frantically clean up the piles of ribbons, silk flowers, and wreath-wrapping wire from the side hustle she had started. This was done in deference to her domestic duties, which reigned supreme. Indeed, Mom's glue-gun-burned fingers enabled us kids to do the "extras" in life, such as take summer vacations and go to camp, but her efforts were treated as mere distractions from her top priority, taking care of our home. Whenever my parents, my brother, and I would go out to eat, the meal invariably would conclude with Mom reminding us to thank Dad for providing it for us. But hadn't she helped provide for it too? It never occurred to us to thank Mom as well. The hidden message here was hard to miss: a proper wife didn't work an "outside" job, and there was nothing more important than being a proper wife. And most of us pick up on this powerful paradigm early on.

If you're like me and have taught school, then perhaps you've noticed that little boys raise their hands far more frequently than do little girls. The girls in the group generally wait to be called on, they wait to be sure that they have the right answer, they wait and they wait and they wait. And maybe the most tragic part of it all is that this insecurity about making themselves heard, about being perceived as just *too much*, continues as they grow up.

A recent study[1] found that when women are the minority in a group where all participants are being invited to share their thoughts about how to solve a problem, they speak *75 percent less* than men do. Girls, and then women, receive countless cues telling them to be humble, polite, and not cause a stir, so these figures come as no surprise. It also came as no surprise that there in the Rwandan judge's chambers, I stood at an impasse. Should I stay quiet like my mom or take charge like my dad? Even with the question pressing in on me, I experienced a fresh strain of emotion that compelled me to stand my ground.

That experience in Rwanda reminded me that regardless of these internalized messages about staying safe and playing it small, there comes a time when each of us is called to use our one and only life to risk big and act boldly on behalf of something or someone we prize. To refuse to act just isn't an option; we simply *must* move. Maybe inviting that quiet colleague to lunch will help her feel known. Maybe our simple presence will comfort a friend who is lying in a hospital bed. Maybe a quick but heartfelt "You got this, Mama" on Facebook will reassure a friend. Maybe showing up for that foster care info session will change our lives forever. Maybe our timely arrival will confirm for that lonely one that we're for them—really, we are. Whatever the situation, we know that it's our time to rise.

———————

I launched Noonday's ambassador opportunity to give women here in the United States a means for standing up. As social entrepreneurs, ambassadors earn an income while making an impact for artisans living in vulnerable communities. Yes, it's all that and even more. Stepping into entrepreneurship pushes you out of your comfort zone in a way that, while scary at first, transforms you into a person for whom standing up becomes a reflexive act. As ambassadors, the women in our community get the chance to define entrepreneurship on their own terms. They run their own flexible businesses, partnering with hostesses in their communities to hold trunk shows in their homes—parties where women come together to style, to share stories, to shop.

The rewards for these passionate women extend well beyond the income they earn: making a meaningful impact from right where they are, empowering women and helping them feel confident and beautiful, providing for their families and doing more of what they love, growing as leaders of others and themselves, and so much more. To achieve their goals, ambassadors must dare to get uncomfortable, to leave their lives of safety for lives of vulnerability. They must become brave. They must stand up.

Just as I would eventually have to get past my anxiety over being "too much," the people who join Noonday's ambassador community must overcome their own fears and insecurities to say yes. And like me, so many of them have shared that they would do it all again in a heartbeat. The satisfaction they gained from having taken a risk was worth the frustration, the trepidation, and any sense of self-doubt they'd known.

I recently talked with Brandi, a longtime Noonday ambassador, about what compelled her to finally jump in. Brandi had given birth to two kids after struggling for years with infertility and realized only after becoming a mom that she had put the idea of mommyhood on a pedestal. "It wasn't at all like I thought it would be," she said during our conversation. "I got to the point where my entire world revolved around persevering through potty training, managing toddler behavioral issues, and figuring out ways to get more sleep."

Brandi came across Noonday and loved our mission, even as she was terrified to take the leap and become an ambassador. "It was fear— plain and simple," she told me—fear that nobody would come to her gatherings, fear that she would never make a dime, fear that this thing would be a colossal failure, fear that her friends would view her as a pest. It took Brandi six full months to make the decision to join Noonday's ambassador team, and even then, it almost didn't happen.

Brandi decided that the only way she'd become an ambassador was if there were no other Noonday ambassadors active in her hometown of Cary, North Carolina. She was new to this whole thing and was worried about having to compete with other women in Cary for hostesses and orders.

During the season that Brandi was contemplating involving herself with our team, I reached out to prospective ambassadors by phone. I called Brandi at the time we had set, and partway through our introductory exchange, I asked, "Where are you living, again?"

She said, "Cary, North Carolina," which struck me as ironic, given another call I'd been on that day. "That's funny," I said to Brandi. "Just this morning, I talked with another gal who is interested in our ambassador opportunity. She lives in Cary too."

Little did I know that I was confirming a no for Brandi, whose heart fell as those words came out of my mouth. *Well, there's my answer,* Brandi said to herself, while I sat there oblivious on the other end of the phone. *Noonday's just not for me . . .*

Fortunately, she didn't end the call. She'd already done the hardest part of making any change, which is simply standing up and saying, "I'm ready." (Or, "I'm ready to *get* ready," at least.) Brandi stuck it out on that call, she allowed her heart to be open to the idea that Noonday might just be her ticket out of all-toddler-all-the-time concerns, and she dove in by launching her business, booking her shows, and lifting not only her own spirits but also, with each sale that she made, the spirits of women halfway around the world. The other ambassador lived just a few blocks from her. They ended up becoming close friends.

One summer, Brandi stepped even further outside her comfort zone by heading to Uganda as part of an ambassador trip. Ambassador trips create the opportunity for women to meet the artisans with whom they partner, and this was the first one held in Uganda. Brandi wanted the experience to push her, to challenge her, to change her, she said. "If I was going to pull away from my family for a full week," she told me, "then I wanted those days to *count*."

And did they ever count. It was in Uganda that Brandi learned to quit handing her fear a megaphone and allowing it to shout in her ears. "I had no idea how stuck I'd become," she said. Dancing and singing with her African family, staying up late with her new ambassador friends, and venturing out into the wild on a safari without her kids and husband alongside her helped her reclaim parts of her identity that had been long buried. "Noonday has called out things in me that I didn't even know I had," she told me, "and I'll be forever grateful I said yes."

This type of living requires us to summon every ounce of our bravery, meager though it may feel, and plunge through our fears into a life of risk and reward. And yet it's so worth it in the end. I know this because I've had to live it time and time again throughout this Noonday journey—not least consequentially in the office of that towering judge who held my family's future in his hands.

———————————

The Rwandan attorneys who were helping us would-be adoptive parents conveyed their belief that given the time and circumstances, it was impossible for the judge to grant an official ruling that day. This was troublesome news to receive because *any* form of delay—even by one day— would put our requests in jeopardy and require us to lay down money we didn't have on changing our plane tickets and travel arrangements.

Not knowing what else to do, our weary group gathered to pray. And then we headed back into the judge's chambers, where we figured we'd be summarily dismissed. As we approached the judge's desk, I considered with fresh perspective all that was on the line. On one hand, there was everything we had personally invested to get to this decisive moment: all the planning, all the paperwork, all the preparation, all the prayers. But more than that, I realized that what was on the line was so much more than my personal investment. If I stood up now, it would allow Jack to stand up and step into a story of family and belonging. If I stayed silent now, then Jack would spend unnecessary time in the orphanage with an increasingly delayed adoption date. I swallowed my insecurity and took a step forward, signaling my intent to speak. My mind raced as I searched for the courage to say what I needed to say.

My thoughts drifted back to a story I had heard my artisan friend, Jalia, tell just two days prior. By way of context, at that point I still had not met Jalia or Daniel in person. Our relationship, while ever deepening, had been built over email. But given how close Joe and I would be to Uganda as we made our way to Jack's homeland, I couldn't pass up the opportunity to meet the couple who was responsible for Noonday's early success and who had played such a vital role in helping fund Jack's adoption. While Joe handed off our two kids to his folks, I headed to Uganda a couple of days early with my friend Wynne, who would take photos of our East African journey.

When I arrived in Uganda, I was relieved to discover that Jalia and Daniel were, in fact, real people. In anticipation of my visit, they had borrowed a car to pick me up from the airport, and after we'd settled into the home that they were house-sitting at the time, Jalia and I thumbed through the fashion magazines I'd brought, exchanged stories about our children, and had late-night conversations that seemed to span a million topics. One comment she made stood out to me more than all the rest. I asked what her dreams of the future were, and she answered, "I simply want to live and not die. Most Ugandans die before the age of fifty-five. Jessica, I want to *live*."

During that first visit, it became clear that Jalia was still stuck in a quagmire of poverty and doubt, unable to stand, let alone run toward her dreams. She and Daniel had no home and no car, and they were living hand to mouth. In fact, their daughter, Zoe, came down with malaria during my visit, and I observed firsthand that they had no way to get to the hospital, much less pay for the visit once they arrived. Jalia's energy was being spent on mere survival. It was sobering to witness, and I did what I could to help when I was there.

Jalia recounted for me how my small, seemingly insignificant orders had enabled her family to enroll their children in school, to put food on their dinner table, and to employ seven additional artisans from their community. "You'll never know how grateful we are," Jalia said to me, to which I stood there, speechless and stunned.

Our partnership at the time was tenuous at best; was this Noonday thing sustainable at all? I had not been able to pay myself yet, still working out of a closet in my house. I had my doubts about whether I should put all my eggs in this rather patched-together basket, and whether my own dreams of running a successful and impactful business could possibly ever come true. And yet when I saw how much was on the line for

Jalia and her community, and how much had already changed over the course of our short partnership, I knew I couldn't stay seated. I couldn't just give this thing half an effort while keeping my other eye on the emergency exit. I had to stand up and put my faith into this burgeoning business so that Jalia and Daniel and Latifa and Mama Sham and Bukenya could stand up too.

As Jalia shared about all the ways our orders contributed to her stepping into the role of female entrepreneur, I stared into her eyes and instantly hungered for *more*—more ambassadors, more trunk shows, more impact, more success. If we could create opportunity for Jalia simply by building a marketplace in America willing to pay fairly for her goods, couldn't we do the same for thousands of others too?

The reality was that in a country whose unemployment rate hovers at 80 percent, something as simple as a job can utterly revolutionize life. With a job, families are fed. With a job, families are educated. And most pertinent to me, as I stood before that Rwandan judge, with a job, families can *stay together*. Mothers aren't faced with the impossible decision to leave one or all of their children at an orphanage because they can't afford to care for them.

All over the world, in fact, scores of children find themselves in orphanages because their parents—usually single mothers—simply can't afford to feed and care for them. Certainly, I knew that adopting Jack would not single-handedly alter the orphan crisis, even as it would alter something fundamental in me. Getting Jack home would require muscles of courage and tenacity I'd never flexed before. Getting Jack home would compel me to work toward empowering families the world over to pull themselves out of poverty so that adoption would be necessary no more. Getting Jack home would help to inspire women all over the country to pursue *their* God-given dreams.

———————————

Now in the judge's chambers, the judge looked at the other families and us with indifference. Even so, I steadied my stance: *It's now or never, Jess.*

"Sir, it is a pleasure to be in your country," I said, stepping forward with boldness I did not feel. "Thank you so much for seeing us in your private chambers. We would be honored if you would grant us a court date today so that we can then go acquire passports for our children and get them out of the orphanage."

To the collective shock of the families, the attorneys, and the judicial staff alike, the judge acquiesced. Within moments of those words leaving my mouth, he ruled in favor of *everyone's* adoption that day.

Three weeks later, once the paperwork was signed and dated and the required tasks were checked off our list, Joe and I, with Jack in our arms, boarded a flight bound for home, our family of four now numbering five. Upon returning home, after unpacking, opening all the welcome gifts for Jack, and reconnecting with Amelie and Holden, I received an email from one of the families who waited with us in the judge's chambers that day. You see, even though the judge had said yes, I still wondered if I had been a little too much. The words of this woman and her perspective of me began to help me shift my perspective regarding myself:

> A lot of the Rwandan trip is just lost to me. But I *do* remember you pleading with the judge to let the families present have our judicial rulings read in court on the *same day*. Our lawyers said that this was impossible, that judicial rulings always took at least two more days. I don't remember exactly *what* you said, but the *way* you said it was so direct, so heartfelt. I do believe that God set you in that

place and time, and placed the right words on your heart in that moment.

Maybe I wasn't too much after all. On that day and in that situation anyway, evidently, I'd been just right.

Still today, I reflect on the circuitous path that led us to Jack, and I shake my head in amazement over the miracle that each step was. The odds seemed stacked high against us for the entire journey, and yet in the end, Jack officially became ours. Whenever I am tempted to play it small and safe these days, I think about how good it felt to get on that plane to Rwanda and to hear that judge rule in our favor, and I remind myself that it might not have happened had I decided not to stand up.

What's more, once I'd risked expanding my comfort zone by a few steps, that new territory was no longer as scary to me. Sure, I'd been terrified of that uncomfortable place before, but now that I'd stood there and spoken there and succeeded there? The place would never be as frightening to me again. This is how it tends to go; gained ground seems totally scary at first, but then we realize it has come in peace. It's like building up cardio strength: while you may have huffed and puffed after doing a minute of jump-roping a few months ago, now, after all those weeks of high-intensity interval training, you can successfully jump-squat and burpee your way through a class that's fifty minutes long. Your comfort zone has expanded, and now you're thriving in that freshly claimed space. In fact, your body has so fully adapted to the new level of exertion that now you have to work to challenge it every time.

And so here is a question for you: When was the last time your heart *thump-thumped* inside your chest because you'd ventured to the edge of your comfort zone and new territory was about to get claimed? If I had to put money on it, I'd bet that there is a prompting you've received and you are waiting for a perfect state of fearlessness before you act. You probably know exactly what it is, even as you read these words:

- You've been prompted to help that neighbor who can't seem to keep his lawn mowed.
- You've been prompted to check in on that friend who just had a baby just to see how you might be of help.
- You've been prompted to investigate the human trafficking issue so that you'll know how to offer some aid.
- You've been prompted to get to know the refugees in your hometown.
- You've been prompted to move your kids from private school to public school.
- You've been prompted to ask for a raise at work.
- You've been prompted to pack a lunch for the man who is homeless and sits on the corner nearly every day.
- You've been prompted to be part of the solution in some way—to show up, to stand up, to speak up, to *go*, even if while utterly scared.

My encouragement to you as we head off on this journey together? *Respond to that prompting today.* Don't let another twenty-four hours pass in which you push off what you know you must do. What will it look like for you to stand up and step out? I can't answer that for you, because only you know your life's ins and outs. I only know that there is a big, beautiful world in need today that hopes you won't stay seated, remote in hand.

THREE

STEP INTO YOUR STORY

Our deepest calling is to grow into
our own authentic selfhood,
whether or not it conforms to some
image of who we ought to be. As
we do so, we will not only find the
joy that every human being
seeks—we will also find our path of
authentic service in the world.

Parker Palmer

I N THE SPIRIT OF FULL DISCLOSURE, I NEED TO CONFESS that while I just spent an entire chapter pumping you up to stand up for someone or something that really matters, I guarantee that as soon as you muster the courage to stand up, you will be told to sit back down. And the voice that tells you to do so may in fact belong to you.

I have found it helpful to name this cacophony of mental voices in my head, and I give you full permission to borrow the name. Allow me to explain. As a kid, I heard my Vietnam-veteran, "man's man" dad use the word *bullshit* like it was an everyday noun, to which my mom, always proper, would say, "Let's please just say BS," Then, catching my eye, she'd whisper, "*BS* stands for 'baloney sauce,' honey." I have named my committee the Itty Bitty Baloney Sauce Committee, or feel free to use my dad's version instead. Regardless of the words you ascribe to it, the IBBC likely meets in your head too.

The IBBC is like your very own inner-world lunchroom table of mean girls, and if you're going to learn to get up and go scared, your first step is learning to recognize their catty voices so that you can then shout back, "Shut up!" As soon as I decided to stand up, walk through the door of risk, and start a social-impact brand, my IBBC grabbed bullhorns. "You?" they sneered. "What are *you* doing here? You're not good enough/smart enough/skilled enough/thin enough/motivated enough to be *here*. Hey, you! *Sit back down!*" While I wasn't about to sit back down, I did feel a little wobbly just then. Those voices were just so *loud*.

During spring break a few years ago, Joe and I took the kids on a ten-hour road trip to the closest mountain range to us, in New Mexico. On the first day of our vacation, I hopped onto a snowboard for the first time in nine years, realizing quickly that while it was easy to hop on, it was far more difficult to *stay* there. By that afternoon, my patience had worn thin. During a hot chocolate break, I lamented to Joe about what a horrible snowboarder I was, to which he said, "That's because you've spent the whole day trying not to fall down. You were meant to be a skier. When you ski, you just lean in and *go*."

Joe was right; I *was* a good skier. So why didn't I just accept this and clip into my skis?

I'll tell you why. It's because twenty years prior, when I'd picked up snowboarding, I fancied myself the sporty-but-feminine type. Cool kids didn't ski; they snowboarded. Adventurous girls didn't ski; they snowboarded. Cute boys didn't prefer skiers; they liked snowboarders. I was a *snowboarder,* then. All this time later, I still pretended to be something I thought I *should* be but clearly was not. I wasted far more than a full morning on my butt that day; I wasted the opportunity to be *me.*

It wasn't just on the slopes that I was playing pretend. Back at home and based on this fashion business I was apparently starting, my *should* story went something like this: "I grew up a fashionista, majored in fashion design at Parsons, then moved overseas to learn about artisan-made goods. There, I realized that I wanted to start a business, so I came home and applied for one of the best MBA programs in the country. Wouldn't you know it? I got in! While there, I met a mentor who took my idea for Noonday and helped me hatch a business plan. My generous parents loved the plan and provided me with an interest-free loan. From day one, I leased a hip office in downtown Austin, hired some of the brightest creatives in town, and launched the most beautiful fair-trade fashion brand the world had ever seen. My merchandising strategy had just the right IMUs, which, as *everyone* knows, is the initial markup, and our inventory planner took care of all the details on how to balance our supply chain. I was also skinny and rich and had no kids."

Yeah. Right.

The *real* story goes like this: I hated shopping my entire life. In fact, my mom would buy me a bunch of dresses for prom and bring them home for me to try on so that I wouldn't have to shop. Thankfully, 1990s fashion cooperated with me, because in that era wearing your brother's clothes was a thing, thanks to Pearl Jam, my favorite band. I graduated from high school and majored in Latin American studies at the University of Texas because I figured if I was going to do liberal arts,

I could at least walk away with a new language. I chose Spanish, and I did, in fact, move overseas after college, but my experience there had nothing to do with artisan-made goods. I lived among the Quechua people in Bolivia and worked for a nongovernmental organization (NGO), where I helped run trainings for midwives. Right on track for starting a business, yes?

I then moved to Guatemala, where I taught middle school kids. I came back home, got married, and then got a job as the assistant manager in the fine china department of a boutique. I went on to get my master's degree in, you guessed it, elementary education.

Following my master's, I acquired a real estate license. This led to my starting a boutique realty company, which eventually led to Joe's and my financial crunch as that housing crisis of 2008 reached the Austin market. Because of the adoption process, I was scrambling for a solid side hustle.

What do you do when you are strapped for cash? You start a fair-trade, artisan-made fashion company. *Duh.* And what do you do when you have no cash to start that business? You pawn your precious heirloom jewelry at the seediest pawnshop in town. Oh yeah, girl. Nothing like a few twists and turns to keep you on your toes. We set up a warehouse in the guest bedroom, and due to a funky 1960s bathroom floor plan, the desk sat *in the bathroom.* I knew not a *single* industry term. I thought merchandising amounted to the way advertisers arranged the cereal boxes in my local grocery store. My product photos for Noonday looked like my five-year-old had shot them, and I did not, nor will I ever have, a thigh gap.

That's the real story, in all its mixed-up, what-in-the-world glory—the story I often hid. That is, until I realized my attempts to rewrite it made me a mere actor in my own life. It turned out that trying to rewrite the truth of my story was keeping me from actually *living* in the real and beautiful story unfolding before me.

————————

Once I began to tear up the pages of my *should* story and embrace the plot of the one that is real, I realized that the truth was vastly more interesting than mere fabrications. I mean, didn't *you* like the real one more? It's vulnerable. It's authentic. It's chock-full of failure. And for those reasons, it is great.

Real life is lived in the up-and-down, not in the up-and-up-and-up. But I was too busy wanting to control other people's perceptions of me to let that "down" part in. When I attended gatherings for entrepreneurs, then, I worked like mad to keep that pawnshop story between God and me alone, because everyone else's narratives seemed to involve venture capital funding and fancy downtown offices. Because I believed that real fashion-industry executives lived only in New York or Los Angeles, I hid my Texas roots on business trips to either locale. Because I believed that people in my position were no bigger than a size two, I never let the camera catch my below-neck reality. In my mom world, I downplayed my job, because—as we all know—*good* moms don't work. On and on it went.

And here is the problem. If I am unable to resonate with my own story, especially the parts I find to be imperfect and unflattering, I can't resonate with the story of someone else. If there are things in my story that are intolerable and unmentionable to me, then I will find those same things unacceptable in others. The result is judgment.

I never saw myself as judgmental, I should explain. In my mind, I was the one to reach out a hand to the mom on the plane with a screaming infant, or to lend a listening ear to a stressed-out friend, or to confess to a guilt-ridden fellow mom that I also dread read-aloud time with my still-learning-how-to-read kid. *Solidarity*—it's always been my jam. And yet for that season of life, because I was unwilling to accept the truth of my story, here I was judging myself harshly—and by extension other curvy, self-funding, working moms too. (Beyoncé, I am so sorry. Consider this my public apology.)

Eventually, though, I began to see that life wasn't a standardized test, where only one answer is right. This meant that I really could be an Ernst & Young Entrepreneur of the Year winner, even if my business had not received venture capital funding. It meant that I could be a good mom while simultaneously being a respectable CEO. It meant that I could be in fashion and yet still have plentiful curves.

I could choose to be an *and* in an *either/or* world. And in my *and*-ness, I could *thrive*.

A couple of months prior to Joe's and my trip to adopt Jack, I knew that I needed a plan to keep Noonday chugging along while I was away. At this point, eight ambassadors had joined me, and these women were real go-getters. We weren't in Kansas anymore; this thing was a full-fledged *business*, and it was time that I treated it as such.

In the spirit of scrappy entrepreneurship, I reached out for help. I started with God, since he is the Creator of the universe and all, and because when you have no money but have minor needs like, say, *legal counsel to secure your new business*, you pray. "God," I prayed fervently, "would you please bring me an attorney, an angel investor, and while you're at it, some shipping software?" I thought an angel investor was, well, an angel, and I stalked my mailbox regularly for a never-have-to-pay-back check to show up from an anonymous investor.

In addition to continuing my hosting of trunk shows, I had added a few "minor tasks" to my to-do list, including developing exclusive designs, ordering product from artisans, enrolling and training new ambassadors, running the business's social media and email presence, managing the website, updating inventory, and writing every shipping label by hand, because I couldn't get my website and PayPal to play nice. Comedian Jim Gaffigan says, "You know what it's like having a fourth kid? Imagine you're drowning; then someone hands you a baby." In addition to a third child, I also had a start-up to keep afloat, and that baby was *heavy*. I was drowning, and it was becoming increasingly clear that I was in desperate need of a plan.

One of the life hacks that got me through Joe's and my leaner times while still allowing us to maintain date nights was to trade babysitting nights with friends. *I will scratch your kid's back to sleep at night, if you will scratch the backs of mine.* On one of those nights, I was watching the children of my good friends Suzanne and Travis Wilson. Suzanne and I went to the same high school and had reconnected on a trip that Joe and I had taken to Mozambique several years prior. Suzanne and Travis had come to pick us up from the orphanage where Joe and I were volunteering for the week, and I remember thinking how cool it was that someone I'd grown up with in San Antonio was now working for a nongovernmental agency in southern Africa, fighting the AIDS epidemic that was ravaging the continent during that time.

The Wilsons moved to Austin several years later, during my real estate era. In addition to Joe's and my welcoming them into our lives, I helped them to rent a home. It was on one of our child-swap nights early in their Austin residency that I noticed a thick pile of Excel spread-sheets on their dining room table, my attention likely drawn by the fact that I was only a few months into running Noonday and was becoming keenly aware that the back end of my business needed some serious TLC. I knew that Travis had a strong business background, and some-thing about those spreadsheets sitting there, all organized and neatly stacked, made me thirst for some organized spreadsheets of my own. *Maybe Travis could help* . . .

When Suzanne and Travis got home from their date, I wasted no time in asking if Travis wanted to meet to chat. I knew that he under-stood what entrepreneurship could do in resource-poor areas of the world. When I'd first met him, he was leading a microfinance bank in Mozambique, where he had seen what the power of making even fifty-dollar loans to women could do for families and communities. But I didn't know if his professional experience since then would apply to the bathroom-serving-as-office world of Noonday.

Days later, Travis and I were huddled over cups of coffee, him pelt-ing me with questions. "What is your profit and loss?" "How many ambassadors do you think you could acquire in a year?" "Do you want your model to be for-profit or not-for-profit?" "Who are your competi-tors?" "What is keeping you up at night?"

Um. Come again?

While I knew that I was selling jewelry pieces hand over fist, my infrastructure was so spotty and disjointed that surely key things were falling through the cracks. Travis had a knack for spotting cracks.

For several weeks in a row, Travis showed up at the coffee shop at our agreed-upon 6:00 a.m. start time and carefully vetted my entire professional world. After a few meetings, he looked at me and said, "Hey, I've always wanted to run a business. Suzanne and I have been saving for years so that I could work salary-free while building a business of some kind. If you're up for it, I'd like to quit my job and come on full-time with you and see if I can help build with you what you've already successfully launched."

It was now my time to pelt him with questions, even though he'd had me at "Finance." (Finance! Now, that sounded good.) And at "Wharton MBA." (MBA! That sounded even better.) But the thing that really won me over: Travis's lawn-care business. I didn't need an MBAer as much as I needed a partner willing to roll up his sleeves (or slap on her ponytail holder) and get to work. Travis had started a lawn-care business in high school, and he went home every weekend in college to run it, which is how he funded his college education. Such tenacity this man had shown.

I wanted that tenacity, and fast. Still, to have another person put so much stock in my vision was both exhilarating and frightening. I was terrified by Travis's proposition, even as I was eager to hand him every single problem I'd not yet solved. (Task number one on my list: printed shipping labels. Dear God, how my writing hand ached.) And so began a fruitful collaboration that continues to this day. It is a partnership, seemingly sent straight from heaven, that was built upon shared values and the belief that Noonday could be scaled into a profitable business creating long-lasting, sustainable impact for those living in vulnerable communities around the globe.

While I was out of the country for Jack's adoption, Travis set about transforming our guest room into a full-scale distribution operation. He'd hired a few of my friends to help ship orders, which were flooding in at record pace due to the coming holiday season, and so my arrival with an almost three-year-old Rwandan was not a quiet, private affair for our family as much as a stage show for the throng of people dutifully working right there in our home.

"Jessica," Travis said to me upon my return after my three-week absence, with suitcases filled with paper beads, "we are *selling through* our inventory."

More than that, still more ambassadors had joined our community, which gave me hope for the future. In my mind's eye, someday *thousands* of ambassadors would establish revenue streams for themselves, allowing them greater freedom in both their personal and professional lives and necessitating additional artisans across Africa, Central America, South America, and Asia who would supply that increased demand. But that was somewhere "out there," and so when I returned from Rwanda and realized that out there was right here, my breath became shallow at best.

We ran the operation out of my house for as long as we possibly could, but there came a time when it was obvious to all involved that what used to fit us no longer did. It probably had something to do with the familiar stench known to all mamas in the diaper-changing stage that would waft into the makeshift warehouse bedroom every afternoon during the kids' naps. The smell didn't exactly boost staff productivity. "Jessica, come change these diapers!" they would yell.

We needed to secure real office space, and we needed to do it now. I knew it. My ever-expanding staff knew it. Heck, my kids even knew it, frustrated as they were by being told approximately one million times a day to "stay out of the guest room," which was now ankle deep in boxes, packing tape, and those marvelous kid toys known as *box cutters*.

In a matter of days, Travis and I had found Noonday's new headquarters, and we soon signed our names on dotted lines to lease our first office space. And while I was fully on board with this new direction—a real business, run from within real office space—the shift would mean a massive restructuring of the life I knew and loved. No longer could I say I was working from home, ever close to my children; no, this real office meant I would have to get dressed in *real* clothes, endure a *real* commute—it was only five minutes, but still—and work *office* hours five days a week. The truth of my new situation? I needed a nanny. And fast.

The problem with my needing a nanny is that being a nanny-needer did not at all fit with my script of what it meant to be a Good Mom, especially a mom of three children under age five. In my mind, a Good Mom looked a lot like my nurturing, at-home mother, with an extra dose of perfection thrown in. A Good Mom exercised daily, faithfully served those in need, and cooked organic meals for her family each night. She had sex with her husband three times weekly, she tucked her kids in with a smile each night, and she diligently homeschooled her kids. She was, basically, a unicorn.

For days on end, all I could think about was how deeply I was going to damage my kids if I went through with this nanny-hiring plan. I saw my options through an either/or lens: I could choose to run my start-up, or I could choose to raise my kids. To make matters worse, I was deeply concerned about what other moms who were seemingly getting it right would think. And yet still, I gave it a go.

It was during Nanny Lauren's fourth month with us that I began referring to her as Jesus with Skin. Lauren took to my kids immediately, she played with my kids wholeheartedly, and she served my family thoroughly. There were times I would come home from work and find that she had nonchalantly cleaned out the kitchen junk drawer, whipped up a delicious curry, and completed a craft project with the kids, after which she had *cleaned up the entire mess.* More astounding still, she did it all with patience and joy, two things I was in short supply of during that particular season of life.

You might think that a godsend of a helper like Lauren would free me up to flourish in my role as Noonday's co-CEO, but you would be oh-so wrong. Instead of leaning into the competent and complete aid that Lauren provided me, I viewed Lauren's investment in the lives of my children as an indictment, a bar I could not clear, a standard I could not keep. Remember my IBBC, that committee that comes to us straight from hell to deliver its latest speech? Well, this time around it felt like they had been slamming espressos, raising their voices to fever pitch: "You are a sorry excuse for a mom, Jessica. You don't even *play* with your kids. Look at Lauren! *You're* not that patient. *You're* not that joyful. You can't name three ingredients in a proper curry! And have you emptied the dishwasher even *once* this month? You call yourself a *mom?* Ha!"

What I needed to do was punch my committee in the gut. What I did was give them credibility instead.

———————

Approximately six months into this nanny arrangement, I was en route to the airport, where I would board a flight bound for Peru. A Peruvian government-sponsored committee dedicated to preserving artisan crafts had invited me to come meet some of their artisan groups, in hopes of strengthening those relationships and furthering our import-export bonds. It was my first official, they-are-paying-for-me-to-come, international business trip, and I was elated to say yes to the opportunity, even as the trip spiked fear. Upon accepting the invitation, the first thought that raced through my mind was that I, of course, was going to die in a plane crash on the way there and leave my kids motherless. If I *did* make it, I was sure that I would pick the one dysfunctional cab driver at the Lima airport and be kidnapped on some deserted Peruvian street. On top of all that, how would my kids fare without me?

This is what firsts do, don't they? When we don't have a helpful narrative to fall back on, we construct the worst possible one—and if we keep giving our IBBC authority, then we won't step beyond that edge of comfort, which is where life is meant to be lived. We'll cave to adding another layer of bubble wrap and miss out on the adventures for which we were made. Instead of edge dwelling, we couch dwell, and I couldn't do that; there was way too much at stake. I said yes to the trip and chose to never look back. That is, until it was time to board the plane.

As I headed to the terminal, all alone, my fears were frighteningly fresh. I texted my friend Jen—who had been a traveling, working, writing mom for years—and told her how beat down I was by the inner monologue in my head that kept telling me I was a bad mom for leaving. Within seconds, she'd texted back. "Knock off that crazy thinking and go," she said. "Your kids will be better, not worse, for having a mama who got on planes and flew around the world to serve. Way better than if you'd have never left your house every day of their lives to meet their every first-world need. For real. You go, girl. My prayers are going with you."

It would take a couple more years before I realized the scripted path I had for motherhood could, perhaps, include a working-mom plot. As I began to erase some of the either/or paradigms and embrace the truth that I was not in control of all of life's outcomes (that plane indeed could have crashed right over Peru, and God *still* would have been in control), I came to accept the more nuanced story that was mine.

The first time I realized I could write a different story line to what I'd believed was a pre-scripted life was the summer after eighth grade. At the time, I assumed that my life would mimic the path of my parents, who attended the same local high school, met during Mom's debutante season, and enjoyed life in a tightly knit town. But all that changed when a church I began to attend introduced me to the Jesus who lived outside the lines; the Jesus who helped me see a world bigger than the songs I sang at summer camp.

First Presbyterian Church of San Antonio believed that loving Jesus meant creating opportunities for people who didn't have the same resources as those who made up most of their congregation. And since access to opportunity was needed most where injustices proved to be worst, the church worked hard to make sure its congregation saw those injustices firsthand. This explains why I, a naive and wide-eyed novice, was invited to go serve in urban Washington, DC, along with a dozen or so eager beavers who were bound for our nation's capital too.

Officially, my preteen friends and I would be running a Vacation Bible School program alongside a DC congregation called Church of the Savior, one of the first churches of its kind committed to racial diversity. The founding pastor, Gordon Cosby, had even marched in Selma, Alabama. But underneath that purpose was our youth pastor's real motivation, that we kids of privilege would see—with our own two eyes—that most of the country didn't live like we lived.

I'm sure there were a thousand things that stuck out to me during those days spent in our nation's capital, but if you were to ask me to sum up the trip in one experience, I'd point to our team's visit to Lazarus

House, a residential complex for people recovering from drug addiction that in jolting juxtaposition was located just two miles from our nation's best-known symbol of significance: the White House. Later I was told that the area surrounding Lazarus House was one of the largest open-air drug markets in the country, but drug deals aren't what I remember. What I remember is a brave African American woman belting out the lyrics to the old hymn "Amazing Grace" during our visit, as beads of sweat dripped from her brow. "Through many dangers, toils, and snares," she sang, "I have already come. 'Tis grace that brought me safe thus far, and grace will lead me home."

I loved visiting my grandma's old Baptist church with her, and so I knew the song well. But never had I heard someone sing those words who *actually* had experienced "dangers, toils, and snares." After the woman shared her story of drug addiction and homelessness followed by hitting rock bottom, she told of a turning point that had come for her, when she chose sobriety and found a respectable job—serving lunch at a place called the Potter's House. In 1959, after spending the night at an inn that sat above a rowdy tavern, the founders of Church of the Savior, Mary and Gordon Cosby, woke to the sense that the bar and café seemed friendlier and more like the kinds of places Jesus would want to hang out than most churches. They began to search for a public space that would be conducive to dialogue across all sorts of lines we humans draw, where people could express strong opinions and learn to lovingly disagree. In this place, the traditional lines between sacred and secular were erased, and people could talk about God as freely as they talked about other aspects of their lives. In 1960, this vision officially became the Potter's House. Its mission and comforting soups are served still today, confirmed by the delicious lunch I enjoyed there on the trip to DC for Jack's paperwork.[1]

The teenage team I was with would go on to lead a day camp that was successful, if you want to call it that. But the thing that would stick with me, during my time on the ground and long afterward, was that deep, soulful rendition of "Amazing Grace"—one hope-filled anthem sung by a hope-filled woman who was defiantly beating the odds of her surroundings. She was flourishing in a community that had long since been forsaken; she was life surrounded by so many things that felt like death. I wanted to know her. I wanted to know others like her. I wanted to devote myself to stirring up the kind of hope I detected in her. But for a while, anyway, my wants would all have to wait.

Each year, I talk with women from Noonday about these beginnings—the desire to throw out the expected story line, the inner turmoil I felt regarding being a working mom, the twisty path that somehow wound up in fair-trade fashion, the desperation that led me into the pawnshop that day, my wild inabilities to fulfill *this* role in *this* company in *this* industry in *this* competitive climate, and more—and about how I wrestled to step into my real story and lay down someone else's script. And in response, 99.9 percent of those women look at me, nod their heads, and say, "Yep. I get it. I've been in that place too."

A woman named Liz told me that she was reticent about becoming an ambassador because she was "fashion challenged," to use her words. She told me of a time when she and her girlfriends had agreed to go out for dinner. Liz asked what everyone was wearing, to which she heard, "Oh, come casual. It's just us."

But when Liz came casual—which for her included baggy jeans and a faded T-shirt from a 1995 corporate retreat her company had hosted—she realized that her definition of the phrase didn't exactly match that of her friends. "They were totally dolled up," Liz told me, "and there I stood, looking like something the cat had dragged in."

The dinner played to a long-held fear—that she lacked style, that she'd never fit in. In that hotel lobby, there in her ill-fitting jeans, Liz's IBBC had a report for her: "You're a frump and a fool, and you're going to have a horrible time tonight."

Any guesses as to how much fun Liz had at dinner? She had *no* fun—that's how much.

One of our ambassadors, Jill, told me that because she was a trained nurse and not a trained businessperson, she just *knew* that she'd fail at Noonday. "I don't have the right background," she said. "I don't have the right experience. I don't have the right relational intelligence. And I know nothing about marketing and sales."

Her committee's report during that season? "Jill, you'll *never* figure this out."

And then there's Deidre, who told me that her fear of standing in front of a group of women and explaining Noonday's products nearly leveled her every time. "I've never been a jewelry person," she said. "I mean, the minute I told my husband that I was considering this Noonday opportunity, he laughed and said, '*What?* But you're not really the . . . trendy . . . type.'" She was totally passionate about Noonday's purpose and mission, but the strength of her committee's voices made that passion fade to gray.

The IBBC is no respecter of boundaries, and I have found that in every country I visit, women are plagued by the same voice that is trying to keep them seated instead of encouraging them to step into the story that is theirs. Even more than that, in many places, there are very real injustices designed to keep women seated. That crossroads where I found myself, there in the Rwandan judge's chambers that day, was a place that others had frequented too. The dilemma regarding whether to stand up or shut up, it turns out, is not unique to me.

Jalia, though a world away, was on the same journey as I was, as she and Daniel began to hire and train more artisans, learn the ropes of Excel, and sink their teeth into business life. "Jessica, I was always the one to stand up for siblings at the water pump when filling our jerricans. I held my home together when my mom left for long periods of time to work in another village."

Jalia went on to tell me that as she stepped into the traditional path of womanhood through marriage, her voice became more of a whisper. She married a husband so similar to mine, quiet and steady, strong and humble. She began to subtly make herself smaller, quieter, and not quite so disruptive, believing that her husband wanted and needed to be more. Daniel, like Joe, is not drawn in the least to bravado and machismo, and part of what had attracted him to Jalia was her big personality and big dreams. But holding herself up next to him for comparison, Jalia couldn't help but feel that she needed to make herself just a little bit *less*.

"The typical African husband is expected to make every decision for the home and lead boldly, while the wife is to follow quietly and humbly," she told me once. "Even though my husband wanted me to be *me*, I was so concerned about what society thought that I started judging myself and pushing Daniel to be what he naturally wasn't— stronger, bolder, *bigger*."

It wasn't until a couple of years into our Noonday journey that she would learn how *just enough* both she and Daniel were.

One hot afternoon in a season of similar self-doubt, I remember sitting with my mom on twin rocking chairs on the porch of my parents' south Texas ranch. It had been an especially trying day during Noonday's first full year, and in a moment of vulnerability, I began to confide in her some of the thoughts and insecurities I faced. I felt terribly alone, as though I were the only mom of young children in the world who was trying to hold down a demanding job. One of my closest friends is an at-home parent who happens to homeschool her children, and each time my own kids would fight with each other or talk back to me, one of my committee members would pipe up: "If you were a homeschool mom, your kids would behave more like hers!"

"Don't put so much pressure on yourself," my mom said. "You moms today try too hard, honey. You're a fantastic mom running a fantastic business . . . do you hear me? You really are. I think you are a far better mom than I ever was."

As my mom talked, I couldn't help but think about how much things have changed since her early parenting days. If you read the best-selling book *Lean In* by Facebook COO Sheryl Sandberg, then you may remember her assessment on the state of mothering now versus then. She wrote, "In 1975, stay-at-home mothers spent an average of about eleven hours per week on primary child care (defined as routine caregiving and activities that foster a child's well-being, such as reading and fully focused play). . . . Today, stay-at-home mothers spend about seventeen hours per week on primary child care, on average, while mothers who work outside the home spend about eleven hours." Today, a "good mother" is *always* around and is *always* devoted to the needs of her children, a new phenomenon that sociologists call "intensive mothering." But this isn't how things used to be. Sandberg concluded, "An employed mother today spends about the same amount of time on primary child-care activities as a nonemployed mother did in 1975."[2]

Based on my own upbringing, Sandberg's comments rang true. My mom loved to play with me and cuddle me, which explained at least in part why she would gather me up at two o'clock every weekday afternoon and let me pile into her bed while she and I watched *General Hospital* on TV. She reminded me of how she sometimes yelled at me to get her point across, which today would be considered love *without* so much logic; she was on the receiving end of a fair amount of sass from me, which today we would title Not Enough Quality Time; and she allowed me to ride my bike all day long in the summertime, with no cell phone in my pocket and often when I hadn't told her exactly where I'd be, which today is probably not even legal. By current standards, my mother—truly, the most loving mom around—would be deemed negligent. Which brings me to the parenting philosophy I'm presently working hard to espouse. It's a little strategy called *chill out*.

I think back to that day on the ski slopes when I retired my snowboard and put on skis. As I taught my kids how to navigate snow, gravity, and what amounts to being strapped to a grocery cart that is moving down a giant Slip 'N Slide, I instructed them to lean forward instead of leaning backward when they felt like falling. "Move *with* gravity, guys," I told them. "And don't brace yourself with your wrists."

It is wrist-breaking to try to manage every outcome, to spend our energy on living fall-free. It's perfection seeking at its most dysfunctional level, and it's a quest that will take us down. That reality was behind my comments to my kids that day, and it's one of my central messages for you.

The more women I meet, the more convinced I become that too many of us are striving for perfection in some way. We're working toward the perfect figure, whether it's financial or physical. We're vying for the perfect marriage, or to raise the perfect kids—good parenting in, good kids out, right? Oh, how we *all* wish that were true.

Researcher and professor Brené Brown said that perfectionism is a "self-destructive and addictive belief system that fuels this primary thought: If I look perfect, live perfectly, and do everything perfectly, then I can avoid or minimize the painful feelings of shame, judgment, and blame."[3]

Now, before you write me off here and insist that you do not fall into the perfectionist camp, let me assure you that I, too, used to shrug off the term. I used to think that perfectionists were skinny people with spotless homes who wash their hair every day, which is why it was so jarring for me to discover that I veer toward perfectionism myself. (I do brush my teeth every day, if that counts for anything, but as far as washing my hair? Isn't that what dry shampoo is for?)

More jarring still was learning that in response to those perfectionist tendencies, I did what all of us do: as soon as we start to experience shame, judgment, or blame regarding our performance in some arena of life where we feel we aren't quite measuring up, "rather than questioning the faulty logic of perfectionism, we become even more entrenched in our quest to live, look, and do everything up just right."[4] What does this mean? Instead of admitting that unicorns don't exist, we try to grow horns and rainbow manes.

Back to that story of my heading to Peru, I discovered that in the end my friend Jen was right. I *did* need to go on that business trip to Peru to learn that I could remain deeply connected to my kids even when bedtime cuddles are missed. And my kids needed to learn that MOM doesn't stand for Miracle-Obliging Machine. And guess what: I ended up meeting two new artisan partners on that trip whose products have become core to our entire collection. Fermin and Faustino have greatly expanded their businesses and the number of artisans they support, and that could not have been possible had I not walked out of my front door and gotten on that airplane. That trip only led to another excursion, which led to another adventure following that. Weeks turned into months, which turned into years, and over time I began to discover that the more I traveled to meet with Noonday's artisans, the better I became as a mom. In Ethiopia and Rwanda, in Uganda, Guatemala, and Peru, I encountered working moms who never once experienced guilt. Do you want to know what they had guilt over? The *lack* of being a working mom. All over the world, it seemed, women just needed a revenue stream. "We don't need charity. We need jobs!" "We want to work so that *life will work*." If being a proud working mom could be true for them, then it could be true for me too.

And that's exactly what I was after. I wrote a vision for Noonday one night in a moment of passion many years ago, before I had a business partner, before I knew what merchandising and inventory planning entailed. I discovered the vision statement in my computer while hunting for a file a couple of years ago, and I shook my head in amazement as my eyes scanned the page. It said,

My dream is for Noonday Collection to be the world's leading handmade, fair-trade, direct-sales company. My dream is for Jalia to lead a movement in Uganda of women who are discipled and trained, earning a sustainable income by producing our goods. It is to offer refugees here the chance to use their skills and earn a living wage. It is to serve as a platform, as a voice for the orphan, a place where women here can have a business and place of influence to the women in their relational sphere.

I started praying that my life experience—random and imperfect though it was—would serve as fuel for the fire that burned brightly in my heart, to be part of the solution to the problems that I saw. And I started unearthing rather than burying the parts of my story that I'd wished just hadn't been true. And soon, a beautiful thing began to happen. My kids—those same little people I was so worried about ruining—began to catch the vision too. One night during our normal nighttime cuddle routine, where I snuggle up with my daughter to talk, pray, and giggle like only girls can do, she said to me, "Mommy, I am so glad that we adopted Jack. If we had not adopted Jack, we would not have started Noonday Collection. And Noonday has helped so many people. Most of all, it's helped our family."

In that moment, I realized that my work had been an asset, not a liability, for my family. Those committee members I'd been listening to for so long? Well, for starters, I've taken their espresso away. More caffeine is the last thing they need.

FOUR

OWN YOUR WORTH

I believe that each of us comes from
the Creator trailing wisps of glory.

Maya Angelou

I SAT TESSA ON MY LAP DURING OUR SUNDAY morning church service, tenderly adjusting her weight on my thighs to make sure that she was secure. Tessa is my friend Meagan's daughter, whom Meagan adopted from Ethiopia, and the next day she would start kindergarten. As I closed my hand around her tiny fingers, I couldn't help but think about my own kindergarten experience. There was the alphabet wall, the class pet, and my teacher, Mrs. Plant. But the memory that sticks out even more than those? It was the playground where I first was called fat.

I shuddered at the memory, especially when I imagined Tessa rolling her yellow electric wheelchair onto the playground. Sweet Tessa, with the smile of a movie star. Tessa, with the personality of sunshine. Tessa, with no limbs, save for the one I held gently in my grip. I placed my other hand on her back and prayed for her, as the musicians started to play a song. "He loves us," they sang, "oh, how he loves us . . ."

I felt her voice reverberate from the back of her chest into my palm as she unclasped her fingers from mine to raise her small arm in the air, while singing at the top of her lungs. I felt the burdensome kindergarten memory dissipate along with my fears of Tessa's first day. In that moment, our souls felt the weight of our worth. Our belonging is not in our bodies after all.

———————

If you are of a certain age, then you remember our nation's 1980s health craze, characterized among other things by SnackWell's Devil's Food Cookie Cakes, a lovable permed-hair fitness guru named Richard Simmons, and a government-funded nationwide initiative to promote healthful habits among children called the Presidential Physical Fitness Test.

I recall lacing up my tennis shoes during physical education on the morning of our school's test, praying for a tornado to bulldoze its way through town so the whole thing would get canceled, even though in our neck of the woods it would have been the first time in history that such an event occurred. As part of the fitness program, elementary school students were tasked with running a mile—a *whole* mile, which I had never done even once in my life—in a certain amount of time. I wasn't sure what would happen if (a) we didn't run the full distance, or (b) we took longer than the allotted time to run, but I did know that my PE teacher meant business.

That PE teacher's early efforts toward preparing us kids for the test came in the form of verbal exhortation. "Let's go, guys! Faster!" she would holler from across the field. Eventually, upon seeing that no amount of screaming was going to make little Jessica Mayfield's legs go any faster, she came up with a new strategy.

"Here," she said during class one day, as she handed one end of a jump rope to me and the other to one of the fastest kids in my grade.

"You hold this handle, and Beth will hold the other. I'll have her run at her normal pace, and your only job is to keep up." I remember being dragged around the entire field, barely able to hold on to the jump rope with my sweaty little hands.

Keep up, Jessica! Faster! is all I could say to myself.

That jump-rope ordeal is one of those memories that seems so insignificant, until I realize how much real estate it still occupies there in the far reaches of my subconscious, all these years later.

As it turns out, it wasn't just my gym grade that was tied up in that experience; it was this idea that I needed to "keep up" in order to be worthy. When we chase our worthiness instead of embracing it, we eventually will run out of breath.

In my own life, I have struggled to slay the unicorn that says I will *finally* belong and *finally* be worthy of acceptance when I reach perfection—the version, I tell myself, that others want me to be. Only then will I be invited to pull up a permanent seat at the table.

I don't know what your jump rope is tethered to, but I could take an educated guess. If you're like 100 percent of the women I am friends with, work with, live near, or encounter accidentally in the checkout lane at Target, then here are a few things that have dragged, are still dragging, or will someday try to drag you around that field accompanied by a taunting voice that yells, "Keep up!"

- how you want others to perceive you
- your past mistakes or successes
- your social media accounts
- the size of your jeans

- your children's grades, athletic performance, and attitudes
- your seemingly infinite to-do list

The women I encounter and the one who greets me in the mirror each morning tether themselves to all sorts of things that forever remind us that we are not enough.

But if there is one thing that seems to top the list for most women I meet, one thing that drags us across the field, huffing and puffing and totally unable to keep up, it is this: *our own narrowly defined and heavily airbrushed definition of beauty.*

The thing you and I tend to give ourselves over to, the tether to which we willingly affix our lives, is the pursuit of beauty on other people's terms. And it's the one rope that, no matter how big a pair of scissors we wield, seems way too thick to cut.

Chances are, you've felt less than satisfied with your body *at least* once in your life. One international study showed that 98 percent of all women want to change at least one aspect of their physical appearance. It doesn't take a mathematician to sort out, then, that only 2 percent of us believe that we are beautiful, just as we are.

In the same way that I allowed myself to be dragged around that PE field by someone else, you and I allow ourselves to be dragged around by a definition of beauty that is fraudulent at best. Regarding the aesthetic expectations on women these days, nobody has said it better than Tina Fey: "Now every girl is expected to have Caucasian blue eyes, full Spanish lips, a classic button nose, hairless Asian skin with a California tan, a Jamaican dance hall ass, long Swedish legs, small Japanese feet, the abs of a lesbian gym owner, the hips of a nine-year-old boy, the arms of Michelle Obama. . . . The person closest to actually achieving this look is Kim Kardashian, who, as we know, was made by Russian scientists to sabotage our athletes."[1]

That about sums it up, right?

You and I both laugh at the over-the-top assessment, even as we live as though it is true. And based on current statistics, we really *do* believe it's true. At last count, Americans spend upward of $60,000,000,000 on weight-loss tricks and trends each year.[2] Eyes glazing over at all those zeroes? Let me count them for you. There are ten. *Ten* zeroes, which amounts to sixty billion dollars, which is also more than the gross domestic product of entire *countries* that Noonday works with.

Whether it's calorie counting, carb counting, keto counting, macro counting, master cleanse fasting, or juicing, the diet-savvy powers that be promise that we can obtain the body of our dreams, if only we try hard enough, and we buy it—hook, line, and sinker, one and all. And yet do you want to know what is full of crap? *That.* That *exact* belief.

But then why do we choose to believe it?

Kim Kardashian anyone?

We so badly want to feel like we belong. We want to know that we are acceptable and lovable, and we think that looking like *her,* whoever *her* happens to be these days, will buy us that acceptance.

The prolific author C. S. Lewis may well have inspired that lovely diatribe from Tina Fey. In his essay "The Weight of Glory," he explained that every human being wants to be appreciated and accepted and loved by God, but instead of looking to God for fulfillment, we transfer this deep desire for acceptance by the divine to acceptance *from everyone else.*[3] Like being pulled around by the jump rope, we run after worthiness, even though we've had it all along. We are accepted—fully and completely—by a God who does not make mistakes. Maya Angelou put it well in an Academy of Achievement interview when she said, "I believe that each of us comes from the Creator trailing wisps of glory." That's it, in a nutshell. Amen.

For most women I know, myself included, the adversarial relationship we have with our own bodies began early in life. Mine started when I was eight years old, when alongside my mother and brother I attended my first Weight Watchers meeting. (Don't be hard on my mom. This was during the fat-free craze, remember? Crazy is what we *all* became.) Lining up with a bunch of women to step on that indomitable scale for the weekly weigh-in makes me throw up in my mouth a little to this day.

Later, when I was in junior high, I attended a summer camp situated on a lake, where there was a super fun activity called the Blob—a giant inflated launch pad positioned on the lake's surface underneath a tall platform, awaiting each kid's flying leap.

The way it worked was that one kid sat on the Blob while another kid scaled the steps to the top of the platform and jumped off, onto the other end of the Blob. The force of the jumper landing on the Blob propelled the first kid into the air and, ultimately, into the lake. In short order, the campers figured out that to get the most air time off the Blob, you needed a jumper who was heavier than you.

Guess who everyone wanted as their jumper?

I preferred to be called "athletically built," but the fact was, I was just plain bigger than a lot of the (teeny tiny!) girls in my cabin.

Summer after summer, I could be found there toward the back of the line, with all the skinny kids in front of me and excited that they were going to be able to bounce so high and nail a front flip. By the time I was a teenager, I had fully internalized a few key messages—namely, that if I looked amazing in a bikini, then I could live a front-of-the-line life and escape feelings of rejection and shame.

That if I were thinner, I could finally belong.

That if I could somehow make myself less and less, then I could do front flips too. *I would be worth more if I could just be at the front of the line.*

The more I believed that being smaller would alleviate all feelings of rejection, the more I dieted. The more I dieted, the more I felt like I could be in control of a pain-free life. But even as I obsessed about managing every little aspect of my physical appearance in hopes of arriving at the front of an imaginary line, I knew deep down this wasn't really *living.*

I carried this mentality well into adulthood.

Upon getting pregnant, I cringed over having to weigh in at my prenatal appointments just like I'd had to do during those Weight Watchers days. When I was about three weeks away from delivering that first baby, my darling girl, Amelie, I remember lying on the couch with swollen ankles, channel surfing.

There on the screen was the ever-lovely supermodel Heidi Klum, walking the Victoria's Secret catwalk a mere six weeks after giving birth. *Wait,* I thought, my brain straining against the paradoxical reality that had confronted me. A month prior, I had seen Heidi in *People* magazine, her tiny baby curled up in her arms.

As Heidi sauntered and strutted and posed on my screen, I thought, *Whew,* that's *a relief. Baby weight must just fall right off a person. I've got nothing to worry about here.*

Cut to the scene of my entering a gym about ten months later, plenty of baby weight still cemented to my hips, and I was ready to strangle sweet Heidi Klum.

I'd been sold a bill of goods. I had officially been Klumed.

Even so, I wanted to lose the baby weight. And, through an

interesting bartering deal involving Joe tackling some handyman chores, I landed a string of free gym sessions with a personal trainer named Jeff. It would take only two sessions before I began to voice my complaints: Why wasn't I dropping the weight like a supermodel? What use was a trainer, anyway?

"Jessica," said Jeff, who had known my husband for years, "you never did look like Heidi Klum to begin with. Joe didn't marry Heidi Klum. He married *you,* and he seems pretty thrilled about that."

For a moment, I considered being offended by his suggestion that I was never going to be a supermodel. But as I let his comments sink in, I realized how unrealistic my standards had been. I needed to accept my body as it was—which now included stretch marks and a wrinkled tummy. I walked out of the gym that day a new woman.

Well, a woman with new perspective, anyway.

While the truth behind Jeff's words had struck a truth chord inside me, I hadn't quite landed at full acceptance yet. At our next session, I informed Jeff that while I appreciated his kind words, there was still the baby weight to be reckoned with. I asked for the plan, the number of calories to consume, the necessary sugar fast to follow; in other words, I needed the *formula.*

"Jessica, I think you know exactly what to do," Jeff responded. "It is time to trust yourself."

Trust myself?

Was he serious?

As I stood panting in the gym, this truth proved hard for me to swallow. The dieting journey I had begun at age eight had taught me that my body was not to be trusted, hunger was not to be honored, and the Lean Cuisine–lined path stretching before me would invariably lead to a new and better body, if only I followed the rules. However,

Jeff's words compelling me to trust myself and let go of my dream for a fitness formula disrupted my lifelong fix-it approach. He began to show me that my body was not a problem that needed to be fixed. My body was a gift that needed acceptance and nourishment.

Several years after those training sessions, I realized I could use some professional help of the therapy kind. As I replayed those conversations with my therapist, Kathleen, she listened patiently and then said, "Jessica, your trainer had it right. You'll never get where you want to go in life until you trust the one getting you there."

Oh, the lies I'd have to leave behind, if I ever hoped to appreciate me.

Can we get real for a minute? I wanted to write this chapter from the height of victory instead of from vulnerability's terrifying depth. I imagined writing it after Kathleen proclaimed during one of our Wednesday morning appointments, "What are you doing back? You are all better!" while handing me a certificate with a big gold star on it.

In that black-and-white reality, I could speak to you in past tense and hand you my story, all wrapped up, with a pretty little bow on top. But the truth is that this remains a present-tense journey. Just the other day, I complained to my husband about the size of jeans I'd just bought, to which he said, "Babe, it's just a number on a label. You're a size Perfect."

It was a sweet thing to say, but I struggled to let those words sink in.

The truth is, I still wrestle pretty much every day of my life with how to receive my body with kindness and appreciation and grace—with how to trust that I'm okay, that I'm enough, that I don't have to shrink to be acceptable. And while I've made real progress in terms of broadening beauty's definition to include me, it's still an imperfect journey. But I am celebrating progress and not perfection these days, and I want you to do the same. Hey, I have an idea. Why don't we all take a moment to go rip the tags out of our jeans, shirts, and swimsuits and sew on the truth of who we really are: size Perfect.

I think we can get there, especially if we go together. I'm going to spend the rest of this chapter retracing that journey—the journey of cutting loose.

———————

One of my favorite aspects of Noonday Collection is that it's *imperfect by design*. By using native and natural materials like water buffalo horn from Vietnam that varies in color from horn to horn and goat leather from India that tans over time, our artisan partners create pieces that are one of a kind in the truest sense of the word. These artisans are supremely talented and unwavering in their commitment to their craft, but the thing about natural materials and handmade accessories is that you never know exactly what you'll get—and there's something special about that.

Increasingly, I'm finding imperfection to be beautiful—*desirable* even—to me. And I'm not just talking jewelry here. I'm also talking you and me. Imperfect is the new and improved perfect, don't you think? It's so much more interesting to behold.

What if we turned culture's definition of beauty on its head?

Instead of the airbrushed perfection, we could celebrate beauty in imperfection.

Instead of uniformity, we could embrace individuality.

Kathleen reminds me, "Jessica, you were created in the image of God. Gravity is fixed, so we don't argue with gravity. But our cultural definition of beauty is not fixed. We need to question it."

I knew immediately that she had a point. What looked good thirty years ago isn't at all what is considered beautiful today—giant hair-sprayed bangs come to mind—and the trends we pursue like mad here and now, we will someday totally mock.

Not only does the definition of beauty fluctuate through history, but it is defined differently across cultures.

In Africa, big hips are every woman's dream, while being thin implies impoverishment. One time, Jalia and I were strolling along a street in Uganda, when a friend she had not seen in a while ran up to her and exclaimed, "Jalia, you have really put on some weight." I was mortified, but Jalia received the compliment as intended, with a bright, beaming smile.

In Latin America, it's not uncommon to see gold front teeth—sometimes even with little stars imprinted on them. It's not only beautiful to them but also a sign that they have enough money for dental hygiene.

As I write this section, I am tucked away in Joe's parents' northern Indiana lake home during our family's summer vacation. While here, I am reminded that Joe's community has traditionally cared much more about making delicious pies than having thin thighs. He grew up in a church that relishes simplicity, including in how people dress, which means that whenever I visit this place, I tend to leave my statement earrings at home. In addition to low-pressure packing, I am refreshed by the unfussiness of it all. I'm reminded that my definition of beauty was derived from the magazine-subscription landscape of my youth, which means it is as subjective as can be.

When we widen our definition of *beauty* to include "imperfect by design," and we embrace diversity instead of sameness, we deepen our understanding of beauty and worth.

I am reminded of a scripture that says God made man and woman in his image and pronounced them as "very good."[4] I once read that the "very good" in that passage is the same phrase used for *beautiful* in the original Hebrew language. Yes, this is what resonates. We are beautiful, we are worthy, and we are loved.

At Noonday, while we have fun with statement earrings, color stories, and trend spotting, we celebrate that a woman's worth is defined by exactly none of it. Fashion is fun, it's a celebration, and it's a point of connection. It can be a place to celebrate beauty of the imperfect variety. But when a woman's face lights up at a trunk show as she slips on those bright earrings, it isn't the adornment that makes her beautiful; simply put, it is *her*. All the accessorizing is a vehicle to express her beauty, something that is already there.

On my first visit to meet Jalia, I remember her peering over my shoulder as I was dolling up for some photos we were going to take of all of us for our first website. My photographer friend, Wynne, had come with us to Uganda for that very reason, so mascara was in order. If you asked Jalia how she felt about herself at the time, she would have told you that poverty had pushed her down on the metaphorical couch and convinced her that is where she would stay. She felt small, she felt quiet, she didn't feel worthy of lipstick.

Catching her eye, I said, "Jalia, you are now the head of a fashion business. It's time to own this part of your life!"

She asked for mascara, and then a full makeover ensued. We have been swapping clothes ever since. "Treat yourself as worthy," I encouraged her, as she brushed color onto her full lips. Jalia took in her new look and beamed. "Beautiful!" she said in her East African accent, as she raised her chin slightly and posed for the mirror.

"Yes," I said. "You are."

As women, we can choose to put so much emphasis on appearance that it paralyzes us from living our lives, or we can put appearance in its proper place and simply have a little fun. When acceptance is in its proper place, we get to go about the work we are each created to do— namely, loving others.

Loving others is important work, and again I quote Brené Brown's research that says we can love others only as much as we love ourselves and "our sense of belonging can never be greater than our level of self-acceptance."[5] It's one thing if my lack of self-acceptance while trying on jeans at Nordstrom affects only me, myself, and I, but it's quite another if it prevents me from accepting other people.

So, what to do? It's to that question I'd like to turn.

Appearance has been the subject of too many paragraphs in my own life, but I have slowly learned how to rewrite that story from an unexpected place: my adoption journey. When Joe and I were in the process of adopting Jack, we knew precious little about the elasticity of the brain and its ability to reframe memories, expectations, and thoughts.

For us, the "aha" moments started coming when we read a book titled *The Connected Child* by Karyn Purvis. In it, the author explains the emotional landscape for children who have been orphaned and then walks adoptive parents through the process for finding familial healing and hope. Early in the work, I read these words: "The human brain is a powerful machine—it can physically forge new neural connections over our entire lifespan."[6] The old patterns that Jack had learned that weren't serving him well, he could unlearn.

As we walked through this process of unlearning and relearning with Jack, I began to wonder: maybe I could fill the gaps with new, more life-giving ways of thinking for me. All the things I had learned, I could unlearn. The things you have learned? You can unlearn them too. It was clear to me that if I ever hoped to reflexively accept myself, I would need to rethink the stories about my own worthiness that I had been telling myself for too long.

———————————

Several years before I had kids, I attended my first hot yoga class. Now, let me remind you that I live in Texas. If I want hot yoga, then technically, all I need to do is walk outside, do a Downward Dog, and call it a day. Why I shelled out hard-earned money to bake myself into near oblivion, I still do not know. But whatever. In the end, I was glad it all happened exactly the way that it did.

At the end of this hot yoga session, as we lay there in Corpse pose, hot, sweaty, and wrung out, the instructor dimmed the lights, turned down the music, and began encouraging us to close our eyes, to slow our breath, and to let our limbs sink deeply into the mat.

Seeing as I was lying down during the precious calorie-burning minutes that I'd scheduled for my day's workout time, I realized with shocking clarity that I was *not* destined to become a yogi. Just then, the instructor interrupted my thoughts. "Thank your body for how well it moved for you today," she was saying. "Direct your gratitude toward your hands, your arms, your legs, your feet. Acknowledge all of the diligence and persistence it showed during your practice, and say thanks." She walked around and gave several of our shoulders a nurturing squeeze.

To my surprise, hot tears sprung to my still-closed eyes. *Thank my body? Why would I ever do that?*

I had spent so many years—by this point, it was decades—tugging on my body, covering up my body, and despising my body that the thought of thanking it caught me totally off guard. I'd always been a *pusher*—pushing myself toward perfection, pushing myself toward weight loss, pushing myself toward an idealized version of myself that always seemed close enough to aim for but just far enough out of reach—but there on the mat, my sweat-soaked hair plastered to my face, I realized for the first time that there might be another way. Maybe I didn't have to push quite so hard. Maybe I could *pull* instead. I could pull myself into an embrace.

I wondered what it would be like to receive myself graciously like that. I thought back on that experience in PE with the jump rope.

Why didn't I just let go? I wondered. *What was I afraid would happen if I had? Why didn't I insist on running at my own pace, instead of caving to someone else's expectations of me?*

I wondered what it would be like to receive the entirety of myself with open arms . . . my pace, yes, but also my face.

My figure.

My weight.

My skin.

My smile.

My style, my quirks, my vibe.

We can choose to quit rejecting our bodies, instead receiving them with a grateful embrace. I guarantee that I can find you some culture in the world right now that believes that the attribute you find most unattractive is in fact beautiful. We can cut ourselves from the jump rope that is tethered to a standard we aren't meant to chase and run at our own pace. We can choose to believe in our worth, whether we have thick hair or thin, whether we have pale skin or dark, whether we have extra cushion or a super-thin frame. We are worthy because we are here!

I attended summer camp for seven years, which adds up to a lot of hours waiting in the back of the line to jump off the Blob platform, telling myself that unless I was a skinny girl in a skimpy two-piece at the front of the line, then I didn't belong.

What if that memory could be rewired? As I reimagine those Blob-platform memories, I picture the God I know scooping me up, setting me up on that tall platform, and whispering to me, "You are not heavy." I look down at my cabin mates below, and instead of a long line, I see a group of girls cheering me on to make that brave jump.

My belonging is not in my body. My acceptance is not earned through a particular shape. And both beautifully and tragically, that acceptance must start with me.

What's that you say? You say you've been telling yourself a completely different story all these years? Ah, well do I have good news for you: *Your brain can be rewired.* You can interrupt all the old stories and write a version centered on worthiness this time. You don't have to lose the weight, lose the big personality, lose *anything* to be loved.

And blissfully, neither do I.

You and I? We are loved as we are—right here, right now, in style, out of style, looking good, looking tired, looking any way we please. It is only when we accept ourselves just as we are that we create an environment for change.

First, the acceptance; then, the change. Wow, did I have that backward for far too long.

So, how do we go about training our brains to speak love and kindness into our quiet moments, instead of allowing shame and criticism in? It starts with recognizing the IBBC's voice as errant and replacing that voice with compassion instead. The truth is, negative memories and perspectives cling to us far more often than do pleasurable ones. Psychology calls this propensity to lend more psychological weight to bad experiences the "negativity bias," and it's nothing but harmful. Why? Because for every negative experience, it can take up to *five positive ones* to make up for it.[7] Furthermore, that one negative experience can change our perspective so that we begin to view future benign experiences as negative ones. This only confirms the negative message, and the cycle repeats. What to do? We must stop and notice that we are building a confirmation around the wrong story and disrupt that chain reaction—first by identifying the lies it tells us, and then by choosing to believe the best instead.

In those moments when negativity is threatening to wedge its way between self-acceptance and me, I hold a piece of chalk in hand and, with great intention, draw a circle of compassion around myself. Inside that circle, no nitpicky voices are allowed. No ruthless judgments, no clinging self-doubt. That circle is a place where I show up for me just as I am.

Draw the circle for yourself and don't permit your thoughts to rake your soul over the coals with harsh words. Speak to yourself kindly, as you would to a beloved friend. Rather than using words that define you by your limitations, instead choose words that emphasize first and foremost your humanity and intrinsic value. In the development community, this approach to the words we choose is called person-centered language,[8] and it's the dialect of *worthiness,* through and through.

We need to reconsider the labels we have put on ourselves and others. When we label ourselves according to only one facet of our multifaceted life, *we regard ourselves as partial people.* This is not helpful to us at all . . . or at least to those of us longing to live whole.

Rather than calling yourself "an overachiever," say you're "a *person* who tends to overachieve."

Rather than calling yourself "an addict," say you're "a *person* struggling with addiction."

Rather than calling yourself "unstylish," say you're "a *person* for whom style can be challenging."

Rather than calling yourself "flat," say you're "a *person* with smaller breasts."

Rather than referring to any of a thousand other labels, elevate your personhood to the forefront of the conversation. Remember that you are a worthwhile *person* before you are anything else. When we talk this way, acknowledging ourselves and those around us as persons deserving of dignity, rather than shrinking so many wonderful attributes into neat but woefully incomplete little boxes, we demonstrate our understanding that apart from our *stellar souls,* our *limitless worth,* and our *vast mattering in this world,* all that remain are mere prepositional phrases.

———————

On a trip to Ethiopia several years ago, I brought with me Amelie, who was six at the time, and my friend Meagan, Tessa's mom. Not only did the three of us visit Noonday's artisan partners, but we also accompanied Meagan to the orphanage where she would meet Tessa for the first time. On that trip, Meagan, who had previously adopted a son with limb differences as well, taught Amelie and me how to practically treat Tessa not as "a disabled girl" (where "disabled" gets to come first) but as "a girl with limb differences." A *girl* first, and one not defined by her differences. A girl whose worthiness was not found in her limbs.

Do you see the power in this shift?

Wouldn't it be amazing if we could all apply this person-first thinking to our interactions with each other? To look at each other and see the *whole person*?

There is a saying in Uganda that my family has co-opted as our own: "You look so smart today." It's an expression used when speaking of appearance, but it speaks so much more to the whole person as well. As women, I know we mean well when our compliments focus on all things exterior. And listen, I love a good compliment on my new haircut and statement earrings as much as the next gal. But how often do we as women express admiration for another woman's confidence as a speaker or kindness toward others or gifting in leadership?

Maybe when reconnecting with an old friend, instead of saying, "You have lost so much weight since the last time I saw you," we could say, "Wow, you really shine today." Instead of saying, "That dress makes you look ten pounds lighter," we could say, "You look so confident in that dress." This is something I've encouraged our ambassador community to practice, and something I'm working on too—being generous with compliments that celebrate another woman for who she is, and not only what she wears.

When we embrace this sort of worthwhile living, *the impact reaches beyond just us.* If it is true that we can only love, accept, and support others to the extent that we love, accept, and support ourselves, and I happen to believe that it is, then our ability to engage in healthy, collaborative, life-giving relationships hinges on our treatment of self. Will we disparage, denigrate, and reject ourselves, and in so doing reject others as well? Or will we choose to own our worth and thus help others find worthiness too?

Before this most recent ambassador trip to Uganda, Jalia had asked if the ambassadors could bring lipstick as a gift to her employees. "Now that I wear lipstick and care for my appearance, my employees want to do the same. They would love lipstick. Preferably red."

So, one afternoon during our visit, we pulled out the hundreds of tubes of lipstick we had brought and had an all-out lipstick party. If you could flip through the photos in my album from that day, you would see a truly beautiful scene: confident women embracing one another warmly, with both familiarity and affection, all sporting bright red lips.

What was really happening in those photos, and what perhaps you could not see, was that there amid those big, bold lips, wounded women were standing together to say, "In our shared definition of *beautiful,* we have carved out room for us."

PART TWO

BETTER TOGETHER

FIVE

EMBRACE VULNERABILITY

When we were children, we used to
think that when we were grown-up we
would no longer be vulnerable. But to
grow up is to accept vulnerability. . . .
To be alive is to be vulnerable.

Madeleine L'Engle

DON'T LET MY EYELASH EXTENSIONS AND occasional spray tan fool
you; I'm actually pretty crunchy at heart. Case in point: *home births*. I know this doesn't exactly mesh with the ball gown background of my youth, but the truth is that despite the insecurity you just read about, I happen to enjoy being naked. I am from Austin after all, where, as we say, we like to keep things weird. Plus, I don't live too far from Hippie Hollow, a public park that is legally recognized as being "clothing optional."

When Amelie was younger, we used to shower frequently together. One of the reasons I intentionally showered with her was so that she could see a woman who was naked and unashamed. I have one too many memories of my own mother looking in the mirror and commenting about how she wished her body were thinner. It wasn't well until adulthood that I realized that my mom was not fat. Like, not *at all*. I had looked at her through her own lens, and then I started looking at myself through that lens too—because that is what daughters do.

One evening, as Amelie and I were washing our hair, she asked me when she could start shaving her arms. Leg shaving was still years away, and with no professional swimming career in sight, something told me that an insecurity lurked. I did what all good mamas do; internally, I flipped out. No *way* was my daughter going to have insecurities. We were paving a new body-image road together.

So, here I was, wanting to say all the right words to wash away like shampoo from our hair any insecurity Amelie may have had. Thankfully, I refrained. It wasn't necessarily my words that Amelie needed; what she needed was room to breathe. She needed space to be vulnerable; she didn't need a feminist pep talk. I backed off. "Baby girl, it's okay to be insecure about something. Did you know I have had insecurities about my body?" She looked at me incredulously. I met Amelie's gaze and said, "When I was really young, a couple of kids told me that I was fat. After that, I felt *completely* insecure about my weight." And then her eyes glanced up and down my body—at stretch marks acquired by carrying Holden, my ten-pound home-birthed child; at pockmarks acquired by carrying all the shingles-inducing stress involved in the adoption process. And do you know what she said? "But Mommy, you *aren't* fat."

I was a little relieved because—well, kids are honest. Looking at my daughter, I said, "I know I'm not fat, sweetheart. But because those kids had told me with such certainty that I *was,* I'd chosen to believe what they said instead of simply accepting myself."

I told Amelie that it had taken me years and years to get over those mean comments. And then I said, "But you don't have to get stuck like

I did. You don't have to accept other people's mean assessments, Amelie. And when you share your story in a safe place, with someone like me, I get to unstick those stories for you."

Amelie told me what had been going on. The year prior, when she'd been making Joe a greeting card in class at school, the kid sitting next to her saw her coloring in the hair on Joe's arms and said, "Your arms are hairy, just like your dad's." And in that moment, that became her story. Her lens.

Until that night in the shower.

Until vulnerability worked its unsticking magic.

———————————

Just as my brave daughter had experienced that night in the shower, we don't truly grow until we own and live our stories *in the context of other people*. Right? I mean, Amelie could have had an "aha" moment when she was in the shower alone, but the revelation wouldn't have progressed her nearly as much as having had it next to me. We can't grow without vulnerability, and we can't be vulnerable alone.

This was the lesson that Oprah Winfrey said she learned after twenty-five years of interviewing countless people on her self-titled talk show. For those of you who were deprived of *The Oprah Winfrey Show* while you were learning to adult for the very first time, I am sorry, because adulting is hard work and Oprah softened the blow. You know what Oprah said she learned from the thirty thousand interviews she did? "They all wanted validation. . . . Every single person you will ever meet shares that common desire. They want to know: 'Do you see me? Do you hear me? Does what I say mean anything to you?'"[1]

We all want to be seen and heard. But being seen and heard

requires that two important things happen—that we show up and let ourselves be seen (vulnerability), and that, when we muster the courage to do that, we feel that we are heard (empathy). Notice something about this equation? It involves *other people,* right?

Perhaps the most powerful demonstration of vulnerability I've witnessed firsthand happened when my friend Norbert Munana shared his story of heartbreak and healing with me. This is the same Norbert who represented Joe and me as our attorney when we were in Rwanda to finalize our adoption of Jack. Norbert accompanied us to the judge's office and sat by our side as we awaited the judge's official proclamation, and there in the waiting room were more than a dozen men, all wearing pink jumpsuits—a clear sign, Norbert explained to us, that they were *génocidaires* being prosecuted for crimes against their fellow Rwandans in 1994.

Norbert is around my age, and as he recounted his story to me, I couldn't help but think about what I was doing in 1994. Homecoming mums, student council meetings, and a 1967 yellow Mustang that my dad gifted me for my sixteenth birthday came to mind. But for Rwandans, the year will always be remembered for an atrocity: the Rwandan genocide. Norbert's sixteenth birthday, in stark contrast to mine, was spent hiding in a forest as a recently orphaned teen.

In April of that year, historic racial tensions came to a head when the Hutu-led government accused the Tutsi-led rebel group known as the Rwandan Patriotic Front of murdering the Hutu president. This event was the match that lit the bonfire. The Hutu government called for an all-out extinction of the Tutsi, referring to them as cockroaches who had too long oppressed the majority Hutu. They encouraged all loyal Hutu citizens to turn on their Tutsi neighbors—and to show no mercy.

In four months' time, almost a million Tutsi were slaughtered. Additionally, Hutu who were found to be Tutsi sympathizers were also killed. Hutu civilians were handed machetes, clubs, and knives in order to carry out the singular, straightforward order: "Maim and kill all Tutsi. No Tutsi shall remain."

When people tried to flee the violence, police officers and soldiers set up checkpoints and travel barricades, screened all passersby for their official Rwandan ID cards, and systematically executed anyone whose card listed Tutsi in the spot reserved for ethnic affiliation.

As we walked through the streets of Kigali on the way to court with Norbert, it was incredibly sobering to think that nearly everyone we met over the age of twenty-five was directly affected by the genocide. The country's countless widows, orphans, and refugees still speak to the painful legacy of 1994. Despite such a devastating tragedy, it's amazing to see how Rwandans have healed and continue to heal their country. Norbert is one of those healers.

When Joe, Norbert, and I were gathered for lunch one day after court, I asked Norbert if he would share his story with me. I wanted to know how the genocide had impacted him. I asked. He hedged, and so I pressed in. He hedged more. I paused, trying to be polite. Something in his tone told me that although he was struggling to find the words, he wanted to share his thoughts. Slowly, with layer upon layer of hesitation, he told Joe and me his harrowing story. Norbert had lost nearly his entire family during the hundred-day horror story twenty years prior; his home had been burned to the ground; his parents and his sisters had been slaughtered by machete-wielding men even as Norbert listened on from his hiding spot in a nearby stand of trees. *He heard his family being killed.* Their terrified screams. Their desperate pleas for mercy. The silence that fell too soon. Tears streamed down his face as he recounted horror after horror.

The night when his parents and sisters were killed, Norbert and two of his brothers ran to hide in the nearby forest. Norbert, being the oldest, decided that they should all hide separately so that if they were found, they would not be killed together. He devised a series of whistles so that the three of them could communicate safety or danger, and for three months, all they knew were one another's whistles. By some miracle, all three boys lived to tell about the ordeal.

Eventually, Norbert hitchhiked to Kigali, Rwanda's capital, where for months he took odd jobs as often as he could land them, which for him meant week after week sleeping on the streets and desperately searching for food. Later, he strung together enough paid work to cover not only his basic needs—food, shelter, clean water, clothing—but also an education. Despite unthinkable odds and unbelievable circumstances, Norbert was determined to achieve his dream of becoming a university graduate.

Not only would Norbert complete his university studies, but he would also go on to apply to, get accepted to, and graduate from law school. Upon being officially declared a lawyer, Norbert knew that he wanted to volunteer a portion of his time to help the orphaned and the vulnerable in his homeland. He was determined to use his education to be something of an advocate for them, since he himself had experienced the pain of being orphaned at age sixteen. Tears streamed down my face as I realized that this man was harnessing his own devastating experience to bring our son home, so that there would be one less orphan in Rwanda. I reflected on the months that had passed—my rushed trip to DC when I didn't know if this adoption process would lead to Jack joining our family; the sleepless nights when I lay awake wondering how the whole thing would unfold; the emailed reassurances from Norbert on a near-monthly basis. "Don't worry," he'd write. "I understand your concern. Thank you for loving your son so well. Soon, he will be yours." Yes, Norbert understood more about what was at stake for us than I ever could have known.

Norbert demonstrated tremendous courage that day in sharing the story of his shattered past. Perhaps it was the distance created by the language barrier between us, or the fact that Joe and I were from thousands of miles away, that made Norbert feel safe enough to share; sometimes our defenses weaken most when we're in the presence of strangers, not those we love. We care less about what they think in the moment, and because we don't connect daily, our fear of retribution for oversharing tends to go way down. I found out years later that Norbert had not yet shared the details of his story with anyone, including his wife. He let Joe and me in. Regardless of who is on the listening end, it can feel incredibly daunting to stand at that crossroads where we must decide whether we'll pretend and present the version of ourselves as we *want* to be seen or if we'll show up and allow our real selves to be seen.

I had spent inordinate amounts of energy playing actor in my own story, showing certain parts of me to certain people. I did this because I assumed that if people knew the truth of my organization's story—that it began on the back of pawned gold and in a bathroom office—they would discount our success. They would think *I* was not legit. But as I began to practice vulnerability when the opportunity arose, I gained confidence for owning my truth and letting the consequences of that decision fall as they may.

I would get invited to exclusive events for CEOs or to sit on panels with far more successful people than I, and instead of staying up late crash-coursing on LinkedIn articles, I would introduce myself and say, "I normally feel like I would need to fake it in situations such as this one, but I don't do that anymore. I am a bootstrapped entrepreneur who has no previous experience on an executive team but who has a lot of experience in hustle." And I would bring to that group or that panel exactly what I had to give—*me.*

On other occasions, I would be hip deep in a leadership quandary, and instead of trying to hide the truth ("Of course I know how to manipulate a pivot table!"), I'd own it, the good and the bad.

Just last month, vulnerability came looking for me when I was scrolling through my photo album and glimpsed a photo that awakened my now-sleepy IBBC. It was a photo of Amelie and me. I immediately trashed the photo, hoping that would somehow erase the taunts about my body I heard in my head. But by now I had learned that practicing vulnerability by reaching out to a compassionate friend is more effective, so I did. I restored the photo from my trash file and sent it to Stacie along with a text quoting my IBBC verbatim, to which she texted back, "All I see are cute braids and mother-daughter love. Don't let that insecurity steal from the true beauty of this picture."

If there is one formula that I can share with you, it is this: vulnerability, when met with empathy, leads to wholeness. It works this way every time.

The more I embraced vulnerability—that ability to take meaningful risk without knowing the outcome—the more I realized that it was the path to the connection I craved. And it laid itself out before me the moment that Joe and I decided to adopt. Remember the unicorn mom who wanted to put perfect parenting *in* so that perfect kids could come *out*? Yeah, that was me my first few years of parenting, but after adopting Jack things were different. Deciding to grow our family through adoption meant opening ourselves up to a new way of parenting. What we learned in all the seminars that we attended leading up to the adoption is that our goal in parenting all our children, no matter their history or background, should always and primarily be connection.

Some of the toughest situations in which to manifest vulnerability and empathy involve the people we happen to love most. I realized this truth afresh on a recent Wednesday morning before school. At issue was a pair of school pants. Or *two* pairs, to be precise. That morning Jack had pulled on a pair of pants that had a rip down one of the legs. We live in Austin and all, but I can still be a little old fashioned. For the same reason that you will never spot any of us Honegger girls wearing leggings as pants at the airport, I didn't want him wearing ripped pants to school. With a ticking clock and a meeting I needed to get to, I asked Jack to change clothes. Except that I didn't exactly ask. *Asking* would have been wise: "Hey, buddy, those pants are ripped. Would you please swap them out for the pair that's not ripped instead?"

No, what I did was more in the realm of *demand*. "You are *not* wearing ripped pants to school. Go get your pair that's not ripped. I'm already running late!"

As Jack stood before me, shell shocked and refusing to change, I scurried around the kitchen, grabbing my laptop bag, my purse, and my keys, and muttered, "You don't want to change your clothes? Really? Then I'll just take away *every pair of pants you own,* and you don't have to wear anything to school."

Moments later, Jack fled to his room, but not to change his pants.

When I found him moments later, he had dived headfirst into his bed, blanket overhead with feet sticking out where his head should have been, and now refused to speak. My anger only grew.

Flight. Disconnection. Silence.

I felt like Mom of the Year.

It's easy to judge ourselves in these situations. But an atmosphere of judgment instead of compassion shuts down the opportunity for us to stay connected to ourselves, and by extension, to others. I decided to change my defensive posture to one of curiosity: *What triggers this reaction in me to my kid?* I wondered, and with my child huddled under a blanket, me now cuddled next to him in an apologetic embrace, a clear pattern emerged: the more Jack would shut down, isolate, and disconnect, the more I would totally rage. This was not connected parenting. This was not how I wanted to live.

During that season of parenting misses (the ripped-pants episode was but one in a sequence of maddening exchanges between my son and me), I went to a leadership retreat where one of the featured speakers was psychiatrist Curt Thompson, the author of *The Soul of Shame*. His talk cracked me wide open, and so right after that session, I sought him out and cornered him as only a woman on a mission can. "I am not responding well to one of my kids," I said, even before I had told him my name.

Curt laughed good-naturedly and without missing a beat said, "Well, at least you're owning your part of it. Tell me, what's been going on?"

To relay the entire contents of what wound up being an impromptu therapy session would be to usurp this entire chapter, but this gem from Curt I must recount. He said, "Deep calls to deep, and sometimes God brings people into our lives who can help us overcome what we need to overcome—if only we'll let them. We save each other, you know? We need each other, to heal. What is the whisper in your heart that you hear when your son is shutting you out?"

In fact, that whisper was more like a yell. "You are all alone in the world," it said, "and no one will come to your aid." Seeing Jack disconnect, essentially withdrawing into a dark cave and spray-painting Do Not Disturb on the wall of his heart, triggered feelings in me of powerlessness, aloneness, and the same fear that I had experienced as a child. One of the bravest things we can do is to be still and alone long enough to *feel* our feelings, and once I learned to be still, *that* is what I felt. Feeling our feelings *is* vulnerability.

After excavating more of this pattern between Jack and me in the month that followed, I came to terms with part of my girlhood that I had stuffed way down deep for years. The contents of that will have to wait for another book, but for now here is what I'll say: it was only by saying yes to the invitation Jack had given me into vulnerability that I could exhibit empathy toward his tendency to isolate. Creating a space for other people's pain is impossible when we deny our own pain. It takes courage to step into vulnerability, but only by owning our own hard places can we empathize. If we want to deepen our relationships with others, then vulnerability is the state that we must pass through.

If you're longing to leave a life of safety for a life of risk, meaning, and impact, then please read this carefully: *you cannot get there on your own.* You—*even you*—were made for community. To flourish, we must work *with,* not against, togetherness, and to prize togetherness, we must come out of isolation and be seen.

Regardless of whether you fear being perceived as weak, or you think that you will be a burden to others, or you don't know if you can return the favor, or you are afraid that people will say no, or you are afraid that your need is excessive and, well, needy, choosing self-reliance and isolation is *never the better bet.* While it may indeed be safer to curl up on the couch for *The West Wing* reruns night after night, that is hardly the life you were made for. It's not at all what *flourishing* means. My friend, you and I cannot serve in a context of isolation. We cannot give in a context of isolation. We cannot grow in a context of isolation. *We cannot truly live all by ourselves.* And so we are here at vulnerability's doorstep, knowing that we simply must let it in because it's in the safety of each other's vulnerability that we finally find the healing we've so frantically and desperately sought.

I think back on Amelie's insecurity, the one she shared with me in the shower that day. For months and months she swore me to secrecy regarding the exact nature of the pain she bore. A year after all this happened, I was preparing a keynote talk for a conference. I got to a certain point in my outline and thought, "Amelie's story would be a perfect fit here." I found Amelie to ask for her permission. "Sure, Mom!" she said. "But I forget: What was it again that I was so upset about?"

That moment, for me, is framed. *She no longer felt any shame.* It was gone. Until this beautiful moment, I hadn't realized how much shame lost its power that night in the shower.

This is the beauty of vulnerability and empathy, my friend. The "me too" we hear when we are brave enough to invite vulnerability in? It heals us every time.

SIX

CREATE COMPASSIONATE SPACES

Broad, wholesome, charitable
views of men and things can not
be acquired by vegetating in
one little corner of the earth
all one's lifetime.

Mark Twain

WHEN YOU AND I LEFT MY FRIEND NORBERT, he had bravely
said yes to the opportunity to be vulnerable with Joe and me
by sharing his story of pain and loss as a genocide survivor. But to help
you understand the magnitude of Norbert's courage, I have to tell you
what happened a couple of years after that conversation.

I was in Rwanda traveling with about thirty Noonday ambassadors, and I asked Norbert if he would be willing to share his story with
this team of world-changing women. This time around, he took no
time deliberating and said in his charming accented English, "Of course,
my friend."

That evening, Norbert showed up to the location we'd agreed on but he wasn't alone. "Jessica," he said as he and a woman approached, "I hope you don't mind my bringing my beloved wife."

I knew that Norbert never had told the details of his past to anyone—except, by some miracle, me and Joe—and that included his wife, Florence. This was a momentous night. Norbert bravely told his story to the roomful of ambassadors, and after he had shared, Florence came up to me. "I was so relieved when Norbert invited me to attend tonight. I had never heard these horrible details—all the tragedy, all the loss. I have to tell you that ever since Norbert shared his story with you and Joe, he has begun to heal. I am a survivor too, but my family lived. I think he found safety in you, and I needed to come tonight to thank you."

I sensed as Norbert spoke that night that there were many times Florence wanted to stop him from sharing, the pain seeming too much for both her and Norbert to bear. But he continued to bravely share, and she continued to listen. It was one thing for Norbert to agree to talk with Joe and me, but for him to go in search of an opportunity to deepen a relationship that mattered to him? This was evidence to me that the benefits to vulnerability were taking root in Norbert's life, allowing compassion in.

————

One of the core beliefs around Noonday is that by embracing vulnerability, we can create compassionate spaces of belonging for ourselves and others. When we realize that none of us are perfect and inclusion doesn't come from being skinny or raising perfectly behaved kids or having the right job, we are able to accept ourselves just as we are. This helps create a similar space of acceptance for others. But if we are going to encourage the people we care about to bravely open themselves up in the pursuit of connection and meaning, it's not enough to tell them to take the leap. We must make sure that when they do, they have a safe place to land.

In my daughter Amelie's case, all the shower-induced vulnerability in the world wouldn't have helped heal her if I hadn't received her story with compassion and understanding. Had her bravery fallen on deaf ears instead of the redemptive connection we shared, she would have found only more shame.

In Norbert's case, the fear that he would be shamed for sharing his harrowing story had kept him hurting in silence for years.

During our first moments of connection with Norbert, when Joe and I had encouraged him to share and made it clear that we were willing to hear whatever he had to say, we created a compassionate space. And later, when my ambassadors had leaned in and listened to his story with aching hearts, they had done the same. Florence's words to me that day assured me that not only had Norbert's story changed his listeners' hearts but that vulnerability had changed his heart too. After years of self-protection, he finally believed that vulnerability could be a friend. Which begs the question, *How can we bring about more of this healing and connection?* How can we go about creating compassionate spaces for ourselves and one another?

All it takes is a scroll through a heated thread on a Facebook post to see that we could use a lesson or two in this. In leading a community and running a business, I have seen three harmful patterns that keep us from living the sort of lives we were made to live:

- We *compare* instead of *collaborate with* each other.
- We *judge* instead of *empathize with* each other.
- We *stand by* instead of *fight for* each other.

These patterns prevent us from cultivating spaces where vulnerability and connection can take root. Earlier in this book, we talked about choosing an *and* life in an *either/or* world—that we can be both a good mom and a working mom, a fashionista and an advocate, a health nut and a pizza lover. The truth is, while there are many things that we *can* do at the same time, there are just as many things that simply cannot coexist. Comparison cannot exist alongside collaboration. Judgment cannot exist alongside empathy. Apathy cannot exist alongside advocacy. The good news is that we can find a way to build these compassionate spaces together, but be forewarned: we're about to travel to the place where the rubber meets the road.

The first tendency we must overcome, if we hope to be a place of authentic acceptance for ourselves and others, is that of relentless comparison. Remember the Blob, from my days at camp? Eventually I learned that life isn't a long line of girls waiting to make the biggest front flip on the Blob, with only one first-place winner. I quit spending my energy on how I would eventually cut in line and instead began to focus on my own brave jump.

Comparison is faulty, unhelpful, and even downright destructive, but it's so insidious that it takes tremendous awareness to squelch it. I took my kids to a wellness checkup yesterday. It was the first time in three years that they were present for their "annual" exam, because minor details like wellness checks drop way down on the list when you are running a start-up. But I digress. After assessing Amelie's overall health and stature, the doctor looked at me and said, "She's in the seventy-fifth percentile."

Confused by this lingo, Amelie looked at her and said, "What does that mean?"

The doctor then pointed to a laminated chart that had a series of arcs on it and said, "Well, compared with all other girls your age, you are just right in terms of height and weight."

Listen, I have nothing against the height-and-weight chart at every doctor's office in every country in the world, but outside of the medical realm, surely you agree that when we assess and draw conclusions about ourselves from the earliest of ages through comparison with our peers, we are buying into the pressing question "Do I measure up?"

Measure up to *what,* exactly? To what are we comparing our precious souls? It's that dreaded jump-rope experience playing out all over again, where we tether ourselves to someone else's pace, in hopes of keeping up.

If only I were thinner! If only I were as successful as she is! If only I had her money! If only I had her job!

I'm telling you, this way of thinking is just a fast way to a slow death.

Comparison is taking your kid to a friend's birthday party and upon noting the perfect decor, the perfect games, the perfect party favors, and the perfect cake, choosing to sulk instead of have fun. *If only I threw parties like that for my kid . . . If only I were a better mom . . .*

Comparison is scrolling through your Instagram feed and, upon seeing some friends of friends on some beach somewhere, thinking, *If only I could still wear two-pieces . . . If only I had time to lie on a beach . . . If only I were thinner and tanner . . . If only I looked like that.*

Comparison is listening as your friend describes a recent win in her marriage and choosing exasperation over encouragement. *If only I had married someone that thoughtful and considerate . . . If only my marriage were working that well . . . If only my life could be that sweet.*

On and on it goes; where it stops, who on earth knows? What I do know is that the longer we allow ourselves to live this way, the more our lives look like an episode of *The Bachelor*. If you've watched even ten minutes, then you know that the entire series is built on conflict, drama, and snark (isn't that why it's a guilty pleasure for so many of us?), which is exactly who we become when we waste time, energy, and enthusiasm in comparison's twisted game.

I can be having the best day of my life—sales numbers are high, my kids all made up their beds, my jeans are fitting loose—and then *boom,* I see Perfect Her on social media and my awesomeness shrinks down to nothingness, right there before my eyes. *I was on cloud nine, like, six minutes ago!* I think. *How did I get way down here?* Comparison makes us feel small, and the smaller we feel, the less capable we are of creating compassionate spaces of belonging for ourselves and others—including for that woman who has unwittingly ended up on the top of your pedestal but is struggling too. I have news: you are not small.

The second tendency we share that keeps us from that compassionate space is a by-product of the first: when we compare ourselves to others, we create a "she versus me" situation and wind up *judging other women for our perceived deficiency* instead of celebrating their success. "Her success does not diminish mine," we often say at Noonday—oh, how desperately I want that to be true for each of us.

You see, when you and I operate as though another woman's victory equates to our defeat, then we can be sure that scarcity thinking has taken root in us, that we're living from a place of *lack.* And it's tough to exhibit compassion when you feel as though it's a finite resource that depletes with use.

I'm just going to lay it out plainly for you. If comparison is your battle, I want you to repeat after me: "Her success does not diminish mine. She is not a threat. She is a sister. I will not feel threatened by her investments, her involvements, her wild accomplishments, or her success. *Instead of elbowing, I will reach out my hand.*"

This mantra first came to me when I was driving home for lunch one day. It had been a couple of months since Noonday had moved out of my house and into an office space. Since work was close to my house, and since I still was not earning a salary, I would often come home for lunch to save money and to kiss Jack.

At this point, our neighbors had become friends with some of our mutual friends. This was during the playdate season of the mommy-and-kid variety, and since all of our kids were around the same age, these would have been my playdate people.

I want you to picture this: I'm driving home from work at noon, and my mind is whirring away. There are products to source and ambassadors to recruit and marketing campaigns to design. There are trainings to write and new hires to interview and a start-up to keep up in the air. I turn the corner to head toward my home, and what do I find in my neighbor's driveway? Oh, that's just my other friend's car . . . She's there, again . . . there to sit and drink coffee and chat. My two friends' kids will play while their husbands are away, and maybe then they'll go out to lunch. They'll talk toddlers and potties and upcoming vacations and all the things without me there.

In that moment, I felt like I didn't belong. I didn't belong at home, because my nanny had things under control. I didn't belong with my colleagues, because I was a mom among what was then a staff of mainly twenty-year-olds. And I didn't belong with my mom friends, because I had a full-time job.

I didn't belong *anywhere,* it seemed, which made me feel isolated and alone.

Loneliness felt like my constant companion on those days. Maybe you're in that place now? As many "friends" as you may have listed on your Facebook profile, perhaps you wonder if you have even *one genuine friend* at all. My hope anthem for you is this: *Being alone does not happen to you. You can choose community instead.* If you are feeling lonely and you don't want to be alone, it's time for you to *act.* You have the power to go and find women who are for other women, who know they are loved and love confidently in return, and who are choosing to be defined not by their outer trappings but by their inner worth. When you choose to be that sort of woman, you will discover that many women like you are already walking on the same path. The day I learned that I had the power to pursue others and create the sort of compassionate space I longed for is the day when everything changed for me.

I was driving home at lunch, as usual, and I saw my friend's car in my other friend's driveway, as usual, and I again felt the usual sting. You know the sting—it's FOMO, the fear of missing out. Thankfully, I had learned by now that the only way for me to feel connection in my life was to *reach out and connect.* As much as my community of ambassadors placed me squarely in a sisterhood, I knew I needed that sisterhood in my everyday Austin life too. That night, I texted four of my neighborhood girlfriends, the same ones who gathered weekly without me, and said, "I've been wanting to get together to talk about belonging, and I wonder if you might be free . . ."

I explained that I sometimes felt out of sorts, what with being a working mom, and that I wanted to learn how to foster a community where our daughters could grow up without those same fears. I asked if perhaps an every-other-Monday rhythm might work, and then I offered up Noonday's space. Every person answered yes. As it turns out, they had been feeling disconnected as much as I had—but I would have never known it if I hadn't chosen the vulnerable path and invited others to come along with me.

––––––––––––

This brings me to the third and final tendency that keeps us from creating compassionate spaces: *the bystander effect,* which shows up whenever we see someone's need and could help meet it but choose to walk on by instead.

It was in Sociology 101 that I first learned about the bystander effect, the phenomenon that occurs when individuals witnessing a crime or traumatic event do not offer any means of help to the victim while other people are present. The probability of help is inversely related to the number of bystanders. In other words, the larger the group, the more likely it is you will keep walking instead of stopping to lend a hand. Instead of fighting for one another, we will choose to simply stand by, assuming someone else will step up to help.

The bystander effect doesn't come into play only in serious moments. It also presents itself in our everyday interactions with others, and it can push us to choose inaction when *compassionate action* is really what's called for. The bystander effect says, "I shouldn't ask that stressed-out mom in the carpool line if she's doing all right. She has plenty of people in her life who are doing that for her." Or, "I won't tell that speaker what a good job she did because I am sure *everyone* tells her that *all* the time." Or, "The emergency shelter is probably being inundated with volunteers right now. I doubt that there's anything I can do."

This voice was at play in our community during last year's ambassador conference, when one of our top sellers, Erin, found herself, for the fourth year in a row, with no offers to join a roommate group. Erin had held some of our most successful trunk shows, was always encouraging others in the ambassador Facebook group, and ran her business with confidence. She had a presence in the community. But because she was "Noonday famous," when it came time for everyone to connect with other women who were looking for conference roommates, everyone assumed that Erin already had someone to room with. After all, she was a veteran ambassador: outgoing, well connected, and surely not someone who needed other ambassadors to reach out to her with an invitation to join their group.

As the conference date neared, Erin once again found herself feeling passed over and left out. Still, rather than let those feelings of insecurity take root, she decided that she would just have to take things into her own hands. She asked around to help identify other women who were roommate-less and feeling overwhelmed by the process, and then she invited them to share a room with her. She turned her insecurity into something that encouraged others; but the biggest lesson here was for our community of ambassadors at large.

Once Erin mustered the courage to share with her ambassador sisters that no one asked her to share a room, the collective reaction was shock. Each woman had been operating under the same assumption—because Erin was so successful, she probably didn't need *their* inclusion. It was bystander effect through and through—but because she bravely shared her story, she helped wake up our community to the importance of stepping up and speaking out, even when we don't feel qualified or worthy.

As Erin's story testifies, we all have an innate desire to feel that we belong, that we are invited and welcome. As my vision for Noonday began to take shape, my goal became not just creating opportunity for people in the developing world but also finding ways to build compassionate spaces of belonging and manifest it across every aspect of the business. I wanted to create a space where people, and women especially, could come together for a shared purpose, each confident that they belonged and had something to offer.

But before I could make this dream a reality, I would have to start with some inner reckoning in my own heart. Truth be told, I spent quite a bit of time feeling unqualified during Noonday's early days. Though I could walk, uninvited, into any trunk show in the country today, get up in front of a room full of strangers, give the Noonday spiel with passion and conviction, and encourage each woman in the room to make a purchase, there was a time when my trunk show muscles were flabby, when I was unfit and afraid. Doing the very things that feel easy today shot sheer *terror* through my heart back then—and threatened to prevent me from achieving my dream of building a collaborative community where all kinds of women could belong.

I recall the first trunk show I held in my quest to bring Jack home—the one that wasn't even called a trunk show, because the term didn't yet exist in my vocabulary—and how fearful I was that (a) nobody would show up, (b) nobody would empathize with my reasons for hosting the show, (c) nobody would buy anything, and (d) I'd remain Jack-less all the days of my life.

When the date of the party arrived, a wave of insecurity washed over me. *What were you thinking, putting this together?* I scolded myself.

No one is going to buy anything, and you are going to look like the kid who had a birthday party that no one showed up for. Worse yet, you are selling everything from your clothes to your dishware. This all looks a little desperate.

I almost canceled on the spot.

I grew up in a culture that prized parties—I mean, they don't call them balls for nothing. We're talking serious party food. Serious floral arrangements. Serious attire. The invitations *alone* were actual experiences. It was a big deal, this matter of how many people came to your ball, and as I readied myself to open my heart and my home to my friends, in hopes that they would help me bring Jack home, my committee was simultaneously ranting, *People are not going to show up for you, Jessica, and those who do are going to think this whole thing is ridiculous. I mean, should you even be considering growing your family at all if you have to resort to* this *to get it done?*

The hour before the gathering began was a long one, but after it had passed, miracle of miracles, my friends showed up. As I took in this community that had said yes to my dream and had chosen to rally around me, I took a breath and owned my truth: yes, we wanted to adopt; yes, we were broke; and yes, to get from broke to adoption, we would have to ask others for money. I owned that truth with both heart and voice, trusting that as I stood up and pushed past fear, I would not die. And what's more, I saw that something beautiful was blossoming. Because I had taken the first step in embracing vulnerability and going scared through my insecurities, I was able to create a space of belonging for other women too—a space that would soon grow into our ambassador community.

You see, even amid the messy uncertainty of that first trunk show, a few things were becoming certain to me: women needed a place to

gather. They needed to feel that they could make a meaningful difference in the world. And they needed a sisterhood. As I looked around me
at these women connecting over cute necklaces and a shared heart for
others, I began to see a glimmer of the world-changing community that
was waiting just below the surface of my far-fetched dream.

With this glimmer in mind and Jack's adoption costs still looming
large, I kept on asking women to join me in creating a marketplace for
the artisans whose futures were now so closely tied to mine. But it
wasn't long before women began approaching *me* and asking if they
could join me, not just as hostesses of trunk shows but as fellow social
entrepreneurs who could launch their own Noonday Collection businesses. That world-changing community I had gotten an inkling of
during that first trunk show? It was really beginning to take shape. The
first of those solicitations was that email from Sara in Seattle. As I mentioned earlier, Sara reached out to me right as I was dreaming about
what it would look like to turn this fund-raiser into a scalable business.
I knew that I would need other women who would believe alongside
me, and within a couple of months, Sara happily filled that role. Renee
soon joined her, followed by Wynne, Courtney, Brittany, Krista, and
Whitney. Soon, despite the fact that I was still officing out of my guest
bedroom, unable to afford to pay myself a salary, hand-packaging every
item sold, and using Yahoo mail as my primary communications tool,
I had a nationwide community of women invested in my homegrown
vision. Despite my lack in everything from a business partner to a business plan, these women linked arms with me and fueled my vision to
keep going scared, because their en*courage*ment only brought me more
courage.

This is what togetherness does. It makes all of us more courageous
in the end. Belief truly is contagious, and when you operate from a

place of conviction, the passion tends to spread. When we own our worth and share our truth, not only are we more apt to taking ever-increasing risks but also *we let others take big risks on us.*

True unity is formed when we risk the path of togetherness through challenges. One of the most challenging times in Noonday's history came a few years ago when we found ourselves with too much inventory and not enough demand. For years we grew at record-setting rates, and one of our biggest operational challenges was keeping everyone's favorite accessories in stock. In three years, our year-over-year growth was almost 300 percent—a number that never failed to make me shake my head in amazement. As we headed into 2015, we placed what were, at the time, record high orders with our artisan business partners and then followed up quickly with additional large, early orders for the insanity of the holiday selling season.

But by the summer of that year, it was becoming clear that the expected growth rate was just not materializing. After some close analysis, we realized that a key reason for this less-than-hoped-for performance was, ironically, in our attempts to make sure that Noonday's growth was sustainable for the long term. We had thrown a whole lot of change at our ambassadors, and it was just too much too fast for many. We had unveiled new policies and compensation that supported future growth through the ambassador coaching program, a brand-new opportunity for ambassadors to grow their leadership and their income by leading a team. Simultaneously, we had launched a completely new website that ambassadors would use to manage their businesses. It was, put simply, a lot.

Travis and I had been so bent on the positives that we had not considered that with change can come churn—and in this case, that churn looked like ambassadors stepping away from their businesses. As a result, our supply and demand were out of sync and Noonday was looking at a future where we would be sitting on excess inventory. *One million dollars* of excess inventory. I remember walking through the warehouse that year praying for the necklaces, bracelets, and earrings to find homes.

As you'll remember, my dad always said, *cash is king.* In the world of retail, excess inventory can tank a business. In the world of small business start-ups, the main reason companies go out of business is that they run out of cash and can't pay bills. We saw the cash crunch on the horizon and worked with a bank to increase our line of credit. When we signed on the dotted line, it felt like we were signing our lives away because we personally guaranteed the loan.

We then took that line of credit and continued to make purchase orders with our artisan business partners, even though, as the mountains of necklaces in our warehouse testified, we didn't need any more inventory. We prepurchased product that we knew we wouldn't really need for quite some time so that our partners could plan for the inevitable impact it would have on their businesses. We wanted to create a compassionate space in our business that didn't just put the bottom line at the forefront but that took into consideration the feelings and concerns of all our stakeholders. That's the thing about collaboration—your fates are all tied together, so no decision can be made in a vacuum.

It was after the summer of 2015 that the over-inventoried situation escalated from being an internal operational challenge to a full-on crisis. Rumors and rumblings began spreading among ambassadors that Noonday was planning to slow down orders with our artisan partners, and in the absence of our proactive communication with the community, some ambassadors assumed negative intent toward our leadership.

One of Noonday's greatest strengths is the power of relationships forged through community, but during this period we found that this strength can cut both ways if we don't effectively communicate information. Many ambassadors have met artisans at events we have held in the United States or on international trips visiting their workshops, and as a result they are often directly connected over social media. An ambassador in suburban United States and an artisan in rural Ecuador are literally one Facebook message away from each other. And this is where it can—and did—get complicated.

––––––––––––––––

Just as we were celebrating the business's fifth birthday, one of our artisan partners shared with some ambassadors that Noonday was going to scale back order volume. As a result, some of the artisans that she had hired within the last year for those large orders were going to have to be let go because there wouldn't be work for them. Even more, she was fearful about what this reduction meant for the future of her business and wasn't sure if she could believe all the data and explanations that Noonday was providing her about our future. Was this just an excuse to phase them out? She was accustomed to seeing many foreign organizations come into her country with the intention to help, only to leave behind broken and unfulfilled promises. Additionally, her business had scaled so quickly with ours that she had not had the need or the time to invest in marketing to other buyers. At this point, we were her only buyer.

Word started to spread among ambassadors that something was awry before we had proactively communicated with them about the inventory situation that had robbed me of my shut-eye for months. Some began to question if Noonday was being truthful, given the disconnect they perceived between the external praise and awards we had garnered that year and the rumors of scaled-back orders behind the scenes. Something had to be done, to lay bare the facts and reveal the company's heart so that we could come to a shared understanding with the ambassador community.

We were determined to practice transparent leadership during this rocky time in the business. However, we understood that trust isn't asked for; it's earned. After multiple meetings with the leaders of Noonday's various departments, Travis and I held a conference call for the entire ambassador community, during which we explained things as best we could. The truth is easy to own when it's shiny and happy, but when it's characterized by gloom and doom? Not so fun, I must admit. Sometimes I felt like I would rather quit than let down the people I value most. What I finally have come to realize is that my quitting would have struck them the biggest blow of all.

The call went well; Travis and I agreed to embrace vulnerability at the outset, and we kept clinging to that vulnerability as the call progressed. We stayed the course, and transparency worked. We told our truth as best as we knew how, we owned our mistakes as fully as we could, we clarified our go-forward plan, and we re-recruited our entire organization to join us in getting better, smarter, and even *more* careful about managing supply and demand.

Walking through this experience together with our entire community, rather than trying to hide our mistakes and just move on, helped Travis and me grow our business in ways we never could have alone. We really are better together, even when relationships get hard—and that belief is the reason Noonday's impact now stretches across the globe.

In our ambassadors' contexts, one of the most daunting examples of harnessing vulnerability to create compassionate spaces involves asking others to open their homes and join their teams to help us reach our mission of building a flourishing world. During Noonday's early days, one of the questions I received most often centered on when I expected to go into stores with some sort of retail presence. It's true that wholesale requests were rolling in, but after entering so many women's homes for trunk shows and experiencing the power of connection, of women gathering together to do good, of women oohing and aahing over one another as they tried on necklaces, I became firmly committed to our home-based model. It's a time-honored business model for a reason; no matter how digital we have become as a people, the fact is that our brains and our very lives were wired for physical, in-person connection.

Something happens in the eye-to-eye that even the smartest app can't replicate. "Siri thinks she is my friend," my son laughed while asking Siri silly questions, "except she can't be, because she is a robot." Well said, Holden. Robots can facilitate much good, but they can't replicate the warmth of an embrace, the knowing look of empathy, or the good-natured jab of a rib.

When ambassadors cave to the same fears and insecurities that threatened to pull me under back when I hosted my first trunk show, I'm able to share my story all over again and provide nonjudgmental ears to hear their truth. I'm able to remind them that posting an invite on Facebook does not often equate to vulnerability and that real vulnerability is worth fighting for—each and every time.

What my Noonday family is doing in showing up, in person, face to face, is creating an environment where real collaboration can occur. In those moments, they're choosing vulnerability, and for that, they should be proud. We are better together—can you see it? We can't win when we go it alone.

Creating compassionate spaces of belonging for ourselves and others is well worth doing, and it has the potential to heal us of the wounds we just can't get free from alone. But even more than that, compassionate spaces have the power to *save lives*. I've seen it with my own eyes, in the shape of a beautiful girl named Hope.

In Uganda, where one and a half million people are living with HIV, many people who are diagnosed HIV positive long to hide their diagnosis, for fear of the stigma that still lingers regarding the disease. They deny that they have HIV. They avoid the topic of HIV. And they pray with every ounce of their being that they are never, ever found out.

Yes, the symptoms of HIV are highly treatable. Yes, with correct use of antiretroviral (ARV) drugs, HIV is now almost nontransmittable, even through sex. Yes, those who are HIV positive can lead thriving and beautiful lives. But in Uganda, the stigma remains, making it a terrifying prospect for the infected to reach out for the treatment they need.

Such was the case for Hope, an inspiring young Ugandan girl I met on a recent visit. Hope's mother had lived a difficult life and had contracted HIV before she became pregnant with Hope. It wasn't until Hope was older that her mother explained to her that she, Hope, was

HIV positive. Although it grieved her mother to have to tell her the truth, she knew that Hope deserved to know.

Hope was immediately filled with shame. She couldn't believe that, through no choice of her own, she had come to be infected. For a while, she simply tried to deny it, to live as though it weren't true. As the disease progressed and Hope became sicker and sicker, she quit speaking to her mother altogether. She was done with this diagnosis, and she was done with her family too. Hope's mom, not knowing what to do, asked Jalia if she could intervene. This would require Hope to practice vulnerability by disclosing to Jalia what was troubling her. But as Hope shared with Jalia, and Jalia met her story with compassion, empathy, and practical help, the shame lost its power.

Soon enough, Hope realized that by pretending she didn't have HIV and by pretending to hate her mom, she was welcoming anger, isolation, and fear into her life. If only she would tell the truth—about her status, about her persisting love for her mom—she could chart a course out of her debilitating pain. Who knows? She might even find a way to *thrive*.

The day dawned when Hope did an unimaginable thing: she owned her HIV-positive status, and she reconnected with her mom. She began to live as though she had nothing to be ashamed of. She started meds to manage the disease. And today, she's a happy, healthy, living testament to vulnerability's force. In fact, Noonday's scholarship program, which was begun in 2014 to help the children in Jalia and Daniel's community receive a quality education, enables her to attend a school where she won't be stigmatized by her daily medicine routine. Not only has her body healed from the awful symptoms she'd endured, but her heart has healed too. She is proud of who she is, and she dreams of one day using her experiences to help others by becoming a doctor and finding a cure for AIDS.

When I visited Uganda last month, Hope came running up to me exclaiming, "I know the plans that God has for me now. They are plans to give me a future and a hope."[1] I want to do everything I can do to bring that hopeful future into view—for Hope's sake, and for the sake of an entire community who will be blessed and empowered by her bravery.

That's the kind of life I want for you, for me, for us all. I want a life of hope, a life catalyzed by compassion that propels us to *act* instead of just perpetually scrolling through a digital life that is really no life at all. I want us to be people who cultivate compassion and create spaces of belonging for those around us. But if we're going to get there, we've got some work to do—especially in terms of how we connect with the women around us. It's clear that we'll never lift each other out of the deep valleys we all fall into if we make a habit of comparing, judging, or silently standing by. That kind of life isn't going to cut it if we want to build a world that flourishes for all of us. So, how are we going to get there? Let's start by investigating a new sociological phenomenon: what I call the *Sisterhood Effect*. You know that wall in your life that looks like an unscalable barricade? Look up; your sisters are at the top, ready to toss you a rope.

SEVEN

DISCOVER THE SISTERHOOD EFFECT

> When sisters stand shoulder to shoulder, who stands a chance against us?
>
> Pam Brown

A LLOW ME TO TAKE YOU NOW TO A BEAUTIFUL morning I experienced not long ago. I had given my all during my morning workout; I had *blown my hair dry;* I was prepared for my first meeting; and, most importantly, I had time to stop by Starbucks without arriving late to said meeting. Against this idyllic backdrop, I sauntered into the coffee shop and saw a mom I knew from my kids' school. Now, this wasn't just *any* mom; this was *the* mom at their school. From what I'd heard, this mom was so involved that she sought out tutors to come read to the class, she led the Spanish outreach program for the Spanish-speaking parents, and she attended field trips *and* recruited the other chaperones. To my endless amazement, she both *dropped off* and *picked up* her children from school. Here at Starbucks, she might have been buying pumpkin spice lattes for the third-grade teachers, for all I knew.

I pushed my sunglasses farther onto my nose and pretended to be captivated by the giant menu on the wall, as if I would ever order any-thing other than my tall nonfat latte.

Two minutes passed, and as I was about to sink into those feelings of comparison between the mom I was and the mom I really *should* be, I did an about-face. In that moment, I realized that although I'd not made it on a field trip yet, I had managed lots of bedtime cuddling and family dinners, not to mention the sushi nights my kids loved so well. When I really considered it, I was a pretty awesome mom—even if in my own unique way. And this seemingly super mom standing in the line in front of me? She was an awesome mom too—and in no way did her awesome mom-ness diminish my own. Before my resolve faded away, I tugged off my sunglasses and stepped over to this fellow awe-some mom. "Hey! Our kids are at the same school—I'm Jessica. How are you doing?"

It took her a moment to recognize a face that's so rarely seen around the school, but soon enough, awareness set in. "Oh, hi!" she said warmly. "It's great to see you! Your office is close to here, right?"

I was taken aback by her awareness of my world, even as she kept going. "I just read all about your company in this month's *Austin Woman*. Jessica, seriously . . . how do you do it all?"

And that was the moment I realized something had shifted in me. Historically, whenever another woman asked that rhetorical question, "How do you do it all?" I took the query to mean, "Wow, you must be dropping a *lot* of balls at home." But this time, things were different. My IBBC had *no freaking thing to say.*

"Christina, the reason I'm able to 'do it all' is *you*," I said truthfully. I told her that because of her investment at that school, working moms like me could rest easy, knowing their children were loved and secure during the school day. "You are the glue of that place," I told her as I chose to no longer define my mothering by what it lacked in comparison to another mom. Before the tears could well up any further, I said goodbye with a smile, grabbed my coffee, and beelined it for the door. I had taken off my sunglasses—I had intentionally approached this formerly intimidating mom, I had genuinely cheered her on, and I had not died.

———————

That interaction at Starbucks was brief, and yet I thought about it all day long. The weight that moment held for me wasn't in the quantity of minutes but in the quality of what it bore out. I had come so far in my understanding of my own worth—and thus of hers. I didn't need to compare my class-mom contribution to Christina's; what was needed here was *unity*. What was needed was two moms, who both loved their children and their children's school, to say, "Thank you for helping me thrive." What we needed that day was *sisterhood*.

One of the things I most love about women? It's that deep-down, we-get-this sisterhood thing. There is something inside us that instinctively longs for it. But as we move through life, we start to believe the lie that acknowledging one woman's successes somehow diminishes our own. As if there is only room for so many women at the table, and if she gets a spot, that's a spot I don't get.

I think our culture plays a big role in that lie telling. Women are placed under a ridiculous amount of pressure to meet society's ever-increasing expectations. Have an incredible career, but be ready to give it up. Have kids, but not *too many* kids. Be thin, but not *too* thin. Support your husband, but be strong and independent. Be feminine, but also be one of the guys. Have opinions, but know when to keep your mouth shut . . . The list goes on and on. In such a climate, is it any wonder we spend our energies shooting daggers at each other instead of going the sisterhood way?

All that results from this kind of environment is a nagging feeling among all of us that we are being judged, side-eyed, and whispered about—and that is no way to build a sisterhood. When we feel judged, we reflexively begin to erect walls around us, to shore up any vulnerabilities we might possess. At the first sign of judgment from others, we either shut down completely or we lash out from the perceived safety of the massive emotional barriers we have put up. These approaches may temporarily keep us from feeling the pain of judgment, but they do nothing to help us grow. And for the wounded, they certainly don't get us healed.

One story from our community of ambassadors perfectly represents a turn to the better way, the sisterhood way. One of our ambassadors hosted a trunk show for a teenage girl she knew who was planning a volunteer trip to Haiti. Mindy, the ambassador, planned to give the young girl 100 percent of her commissions from that show to help her meet her goal, but at the last minute the teen's so-called friends decided to play a mean-girl trick on her and collectively not show up.

As Mindy came home from the trunk show depleted and enraged, she reached out to our community via Facebook to vent and find solace. What she got in return, though, was much more than solace. Her ambassador sisters rallied together and began placing orders for this teenager's trunk show. "Let's show her that love and sisterhood wins," wrote one ambassador after placing an order. Mindy soon received orders from women all over the United States—women who would not receive a commission on these orders—along with private messages asking her to pass on words of encouragement to the teen. And that

no-one-came-to-my-party trunk show ended up grossing six grand. I
have named this sociological phenomenon—how women come together in beautiful ways to see each other flourish—the Sisterhood
Effect, and I hope Amelie will be studying it in depth during her Sociology 101 class someday.

The Sisterhood Effect happens when women refuse to let perceived
threats strangle our relationships, when we let empathy triumph over
judgment and let collaboration win over comparison. One of the high-
stakes ways I have seen this type of sisterhood in action is in the lives of
Wideleine and Ginny.

Ten years ago in Port-au-Prince, Haiti, Wideleine was desperate. She
was living in poverty, she was alone, and she was pregnant. Faced with
these seemingly insurmountable obstacles, her father encouraged her to
make the decision to place her newborn daughter up for adoption.

That baby would be adopted by an American woman named
Ginny.

Fast-forward a decade later, and today Wideleine is an assistant
manager at the workshop where our beautiful Haitian styles are made.
Since relinquishing her baby daughter more than ten years ago, Wideleine has given birth to two sons, whom she was able to keep and care
for because of her job. With her earnings, she has even been able to
become a landowner—a rare thing in Haiti and a source of great pride.

After working in the workshop for some time, Wideleine developed a relationship with Chandler, the woman who runs our partner
business there. Wideleine had known that her daughter had been adopted by a loving American family, but she expressed to Chandler that
she wanted to be in more regular contact with this family. Chandler
was able to reach out to Ginny, the baby's adoptive mother, to ask if she
would consider meeting Wideleine someday.

To Chandler's question, Ginny said yes. She could have uttered any of a thousand declines, and yet in response, she simply said yes.

I would love to meet Wideleine.

I would love to honor Wideleine.

This woman isn't a threat to me; she's a collaborator, a sister, a friend.

The two women did connect by email in the end, which settled one of Wideleine's long-standing, deep-seated fears—the fear that she would never know what had become of her daughter. Back in her darkest moment, Wideleine had tucked the one photograph she had of her baby girl into her Bible and whispered a prayer: "Please, God, if my daughter ever gets adopted, let it be by a wonderful mom."

In connecting with Ginny, Wideleine knew that God had answered her heartfelt prayer. I recently asked if Ginny would share a letter she wrote for Wideleine on my podcast, *Going Scared*. The letter goes like this:

> There is so much about our lives that we do not get to choose;
> where we are born and into what circumstances. We like to
> believe that we control our own lives and we do, but only within
> a larger framework of possibilities and limitations. It is our
> struggle to reach for the possibilities and overcome the limita-
> tions that come to define who we are. Who you are is a strong
> and beautiful young woman. Wideleine, I feel that I have your
> trust to raise this daughter that we share. I so look forward to
> the day when I can bring her back and see you get to know each
> other again. I look forward to the hugs, stories, sadness, and joy
> that we will all share.

Reading Wideleine and Ginny's story of hearts broken and hearts healed, it is immediately clear that being a sister who shoulders others is well worth it. So why, I constantly find myself asking, do we ever opt for the alternative? The alternative consists of choosing judgment and blame over grace and connection, and it ensures that we remain standing on the sidelines of our sisters' lives instead of stepping forward and giving them a boost.

I know it's hard to admit, but we all fall prey to this judgmental way of thinking. And while there are many things we *can* do at the same time (work and be a doting mom, be sporty and stylish, love queso and drink kombucha), there are just as many things we can't do simultaneously. For instance, we can't be both empathetic and judgmental, so those judgy ways will have to go.

Harsh judgment—known in academic circles as piety, egotism, *being catty*—often rears its ugly head when we are caught in a cycle of shame. Shamed people shame people, which is why it is utterly impossible to hold compassion for another individual when we're operating from a place of shame.

Remember the infamous ripped-pants incident between me and my son Jack? Whenever Jack flew into isolation mode and I raged, it was a safe bet that I was still stuck in the spin cycle of shame. I felt shame, and so I shamed my son, which only compounded the shame I felt. We shame others for everything from being on their iPhones while the kids play on the playground, to being "shallow enough" to own big houses, to being blond and thus *obviously* an airhead. (After completing my master's thesis, a professor confessed to me, "I thought you were just another pretty girl, until I read your thesis." I remember thinking, *Well, at least she was honest.*)

Judgment also shows up as a form of self-protection. We shame people for not having flood insurance during a crisis like Hurricane Harvey. When we hear of a sexual assault, our first thought is often, *I wonder what she was wearing or where she was walking*. A child gets hit by a car, and we assume the mom was negligent. We want to believe that we are immune from certain painful life experiences, because that helps us feel more in control over our bubble-wrapped lives. So we distance ourselves from the pain of other people's suffering with critical thoughts, which only serves to keep us at arm's length from others.

One way I have seen this sort of distancing at work is how we often view those living in extreme poverty. When we come across people who differ from us culturally, geographically, and socioeconomically, we want so badly to believe that they experience pain, loss, and suffering differently from us. "Oh, that's so sad! But they probably have just come to *expect* life to be like that. They don't fear what I fear or dream like I tend to dream." It's hard to embrace the truth that Norbert experiences pain *exactly like I do*, as his pain stems from hearing most of his family die by machete.

If my experiences with people living in poverty have taught me anything, it's that at the end of the day, we *all want the same things*—to be seen, to be accepted, to be known, to be loved. We want wholeness. We want connection. We want *hope*. Yes, we want safety for ourselves and our families, access to healthcare and a good education. But we also want birthday cakes for our children, a morning kiss from our partner, and an outfit we can always pull on to make us feel like a million bucks.

We extend the circle of compassion we have drawn around ourselves to include others when we embrace this vulnerable truth: *It could have been me*. When we bravely choose to empathize with people who are in painful circumstances, rather than judge them, we become not only a balm for their souls but a dose of courage for our own. We come to realize that yes, we may all be vulnerable to pain, but if we keep showing up for one another during that pain, we will find the courage to weather what comes.

And it's not just in the big and newsworthy moments that we can find the courage to choose empathy and closeness over judgment and distance; it's in our everyday lives too, as we navigate our relationships with the people around us. I recently reached out to a group of women and asked them to share the situations where they found themselves reacting with judgment instead of empathy—and how they're working to rectify that line of thinking.

In response, they shared with both sheepishness and great vulnerability what they've caught themselves side-eyeing.

I sometimes judge people who drive fancy cars as being pretentious and trying to prove themselves. Yikes.

I used to judge parents who allowed their small children to watch a show on a phone while waiting at a restaurant for dinner. Now with a two-year-old surprise baby of my own, I realize that sometimes *Paw Patrol* is our only option.

I have a hard time not judging when people can't "afford" bills but always have an iPhone, beer, cigarettes, a nice bag, and a car. It's something I have been working on for years—seeing a need and meeting it without trying to fix them or figure out why they are in this situation. I know it's not mine to judge.

I have totally been guilty of judging people for not being positive enough, happy enough, or taking charge of their own lives enough. I couldn't understand why people wouldn't pull themselves out of depression or other sadness. It wasn't until I went through a massive season of depression, trauma, and heartache myself that I learned to be more comfortable with grief and sadness and not just try to shoo it away.

I judge someone who can scarf a whole pizza and not gain an ounce, whereas I merely *sniff* a slice and then can't button my jeans. I've struggled with my weight since my early twenties and have just now, at forty-eight, found what works for me—and it's going great. Still, I'm learning to let her have her pizza; and I can too . . . just not the whole thing.

As for me, one thing I have been guilty of—don't laugh—is judging people who have the audacity to write a book. Along the way, my default reaction to the news that someone I was acquainted with was putting pen to paper was, *What could she possibly have to say that hasn't been said already?* Harsh, right? Clearly, I have turned over a new leaf and have fully embraced the irony of writing a book of my own. I have come to understand that writing isn't about saying something brand new as much as it's about bravely sharing your story such that it will resonate with someone and inspire her to rethink her own.

———————

Often we judge people because of a lack of understanding about our differences. But what if instead of seeing those differences as walls dividing us, we saw them as opportunities to expand our world? To grow in mercy and grace as we navigate the things we used to respond to with judgment?

Recently, I was at a shoe store and crossed paths with a woman who was wearing a head covering, a hijab. She was shopping with a four-year-old and a two-year-old who, in my professional mommy opinion, were not behaving as children ought. (Insert eye roll here.) The four-year-old was busy pushing the two-year-old around in her stroller, which he would periodically slam into whatever wall or ankle-sock display got in his way. Each time there was a crash, I glanced over to see that every person in the store was rolling their eyes.

I, too, found myself giving way to judgy thoughts, until I remembered that on any other day, *it could have been me.* After all, I was about to purchase ten pairs of shoes for my kids to try on at home to avoid shopping with them in public. I went over to the two-year-old, who was starting to fuss, and said, "Hey, there! Want to play with my shoebox?" The mom spoke to me in hesitant English, and I proceeded to ask where she was from. "I am from Egypt," she told me with a shy smile. "We have only been in the US for four months."

In that moment, I was glad that I had opted for compassion instead of judgment. This mama was doing the best she could, just as I was. She was going through a major life transition with two little ones and was even managing to get new shoes on their wiggly little feet.

We need each other, sisters. If we're going to build a world that flourishes, we have to look at other women with compassion instead of judgment. And once we make that commitment—to embrace rather than side-eye each other—we might find that the things that once seemed so different don't need to divide us. Instead, they can shape us into more loving and wise and adventurous people who don't shy away from others but instead rise to meet them, differences and all.

What it comes down to is this: there are two ways to approach people in this one precious life, and only one of them is worth doing. You can either judge, condemn, disregard, and indict people, deciding that they're shallow, an inconvenience, a mess; or you can learn about, affirm, celebrate, and love them, offering them compassion at every turn. You can choose to assume positive intent—to assume that someone is doing the best she can, instead of jumping to the conclusion that she is acting out of malice or laziness or a sense of superiority.

I recently sat down with Addis, a brave Ethiopian woman who had left a life of prostitution to pursue a life of hard-won freedom. She had been brainwashed into believing that she was worth only what a man would pay for her. She had no job skills, no opportunities, and no hope for herself or her baby son. But then she decided to change her story and began artisan training for one of the jewelry makers Noonday partners with.

Despite her bravery in embarking on this new life, Addis didn't feel successful at first; in fact, because of her slow jewelry-making pace, she felt sure she'd soon be back on the streets. But that's not at all what went down. Instead of firing her, the staff encouraged her. Instead of judging her for not being able to keep up, they spent extra time training her. And as they continued to tell her that she was worth it, she finally began to believe it herself.

Addis's story is one that never fails to reset my perspective. Our business partners in Ethiopia face incredible challenges as they work with these women—many of whom have been told their whole lives that they are worthless. The work of helping bring these women out of the darkness is so valuable and needed. But make no mistake, it's *hard.*

It's not all happy tears and redemption stories and gratitude. It's a long journey toward rewriting the stories that the women have been telling themselves for decades. Many of them have no idea how to have a reliable job where they must show up on time and work as a team each day. They don't understand how to receive kindness from others instead of judgment. They want to start new lives, but the business of starting a new life is a steep uphill battle. And our partners walk with them each step of the way, responding with grace when the women lash out at them and with patience when they simply don't show up. They might have cause for judgment, but instead they practice radical compassion, and it is that compassion that is changing lives.

If you struggle with a judgmental spirit, then please think of Addis—or Ginny and Wideleine. While judgment can heap a heavy weight onto a person's shoulders, acceptance can lift it right off. Think, *I won't feel sorry for this person or cast blame upon her. Instead, I will see myself in her, and with great empathy I'll work from there.* When someone you know makes a misstep and fears retribution, show up for her with flowers instead. And when she is over the moon because life seems to be going her way, celebrate her success and lift a congratulatory glass. By our words and by our actions, may we all be women who let other women know that they're honored, valued, and loved.

This Sisterhood Effect I've been speaking of says, "I'm in. I'm here. I see you. I see your need, and I'm not leaving until you are helped," and once we welcome it in, it has the power to bring beautiful chaos to our lives.

In my early days with Noonday, opportunities to witness the Sisterhood Effect at work were plentiful. One story that always makes me marvel involves a group of tightly knit women in Rwanda—and how our collective willingness to take a chance on one another sparked something truly life changing for us all.

During the early days of the adoption process, I reached out to my friend Jennifer, the Rwandan resident who had facilitated Jack's adoption process, with a simple question, "Do you know any women who can sew? I am looking for a group to produce future Noonday packaging. I am thinking about a small drawstring bag. Let me know if anyone comes to mind."

Even though the business at the time consisted only of five brand-new ambassadors, a recent college graduate who helped a few hours a week mailing packages, and me, I wanted Noonday accessories to arrive in packaging that befit the contents—something handmade and special.

Jennifer replied within the hour. "Jessica," her reply read, "just go with me here. I do know of a few established sewing groups, but I also know amazing women here in my own neighborhood who are badly in need of jobs. They are living in poverty and simply need an opportunity. Would you consider giving them a chance?"

Jennifer went on to explain that most of the women she was referring to were genocide survivors, women who had fled the country as refugees. Some of these women had taken in the orphaned children of their relatives, even though they could barely feed their own kids, and now they were caring for an entire *village*, after so many parents had been killed.

"They are driven," Jennifer said. "They are determined to support themselves. Yes, they need skills training, but they could definitely learn to sew."

My initial reaction was fear. This all happened as Travis was about to sign on the dotted line to risk his livelihood on me, and now these women would be doing the same thing? There were *twelve* of these women. Which meant I had twelve huge opportunities to fail. What if they went through sewing school and Noonday was not even in business by the time they finished? I had no inkling how to sew. Where would I find a designer who could work with them? What if the costs of the packaging were not sustainable in the long term for Noonday? Even so, I found myself asking, *What if we could make this thing work?*

I sat at my laptop for quite some time, staring at the words I'd typed: "I'm in, Jennifer. I want to do this. Let's figure out a way to make this work."

When the time came for Joe and me to make our trek to Rwanda for the final leg of the adoption journey, Jennifer suggested that I come and meet the women and cast vision for their future careers. Meeting Jack was certainly the highlight of that trip, but meeting those twelve beautiful women was a close second.

As I scanned their faces, I thought about Jack's mom, the most important woman I would never know. As afraid as I was to commit to these women, and as skeptical as they were to leave their household duties, commit to the sewing classes, and supplement part of the costs that Noonday customers had offered to pay for, the risk to do *nothing* felt much greater than the risk to do *something.* No, this was exactly what I had signed up for all those months prior when I had hauled out Jalia's paper bead jewelry and set it up for that first trunk show. The vision I was pursuing wasn't only about Jack. It was also about creating opportunities for women just like this. It was about creating a compassionate space where *all* of us could thrive. It was about sisterhood.

"Ladies, we're going to find you the training and the work that you need," I told them, steadily meeting each of their gazes. "We're in this together now."

Rwanda soon became a proving ground for the Sisterhood Effect's transformative power once more, this time in the form of a woman named Denise DeMarchis, founder of the clothing company Matilda Jane, another direct-sales organization.

Soon after I'd confirmed Noonday's arrangement with that seamstress group in Rwanda, the women began sewing school. They were perhaps halfway through their classes when I received an email from Denise, who had gotten wind of Noonday. While she could have seen us as competitors in the direct-sales space, battling it out for access to women's hearts and homes, she instead told me that she loved what we were doing—and that she wanted to be involved. Sisterhood at its finest.

Eight weeks later, an entire team of Matilda Jane designers boarded a flight bound for Rwanda, where they would create our co-branded line. And as a result, when May rolled around and those seamstresses graduated, they were handed a four-thousand-piece order to crank out, which is more than some artisan groups produce over years.

On my last visit to Rwanda, I visited the home of Grace, one of those original seamstresses. With now three years under her belt sewing for Noonday Collection, she walked me through her home and proudly pointed out things that hadn't been there prior to her sewing job. She pointed at the tin roof, which had once been straw that didn't protect the home from the rains. She pointed to a water well that provided her family with fresh water, where before she had to walk for miles to the nearest well.

My friend Jennifer had responded to my four-sentence email saying "Do you know any women who can sew?" by linking arms with me and with the twelve women who now had sustainable livelihoods.

When Denise from Matilda Jane heard of this little start-up called Noonday, she determined to choose collaboration over competition and link arms with me too, even though her company was at least a thousand percent bigger than mine. Ambassadors then linked arms with me to create a marketplace for these determined Rwandan women, and women in turn opened up their homes for all. I had known this truth in my head for years, but after my experience in Rwanda, I came to know it deep in my bones: when faced with the decision of whether to go the way of petty competition or open-hearted collaboration, collaboration wins every time.

An even higher-stakes example of how the Sisterhood Effect squelches the bystander effect can be found in Jalia's life. In Uganda, gender-based violence is a tragic cultural norm. As many little Ugandan girls grow up, they are told that they are worthless and useless, just because they are not boys. This was exactly what Jalia experienced as she was raised in the village of her youth, and yet Jalia was never the "sweet silent type," the kind of child to simply comply. She had a big personality, a big laugh, and big ideas about who she wanted to be. And as she learned to own her worth, she'd set an example for other women to live the life of their dreams too.

After Jalia's jewelry-making business began to take off, she needed additional artisans for her team. One of the women she hired, Nakato, was clearly living in distress. Nakato would show up to work with fresh bruises on her face and body, and there was a certain sorrow etched on her face. Jalia knew that domestic violence was a common issue, but what was she to do?

One morning, when Nakato surfaced with her eyes having been nearly punched shut, Jalia decided she'd had enough. She was tired of waiting for someone else to change the culture of her country. She was tired of seeing women she loved being mistreated. She was tired of biting her tongue. And so she rallied her courage, she marched down to the police station and informed the man on duty there that a violent crime had taken place against one of her workers, and she demanded that the offender be arrested. "You will help this woman!" she cried.

The police in Uganda are notoriously corrupt. There are good officers, to be sure, but in general police culture in Uganda operates on bribes. Jalia didn't have funds to bribe the police. But she had something else: tenacity. She resolved in her heart that she would show up at the police station every day until justice was served.

Jalia's pleas fell on deaf ears that first day, and again on day two. On day three, she had to miss a fellow artisan's wedding, because she'd already committed herself to be at the station, fighting on behalf of her friend. Day after day, Jalia surfaced, determined to get her way, and she was continually swatted away as nothing more than a pesky fly.

Eventually, the police on duty couldn't ignore Jalia anymore. Eventually, Nakato's husband was arrested, and eventually, he went to jail.

Nakato and her children are safe today. They are free from horrifying abuse. And they have Jalia to thank for that, their sister who just wouldn't stand by.

At its core the Sisterhood Effect says, "I will own my power, the power that compels me to not stand by but to stand up and reach out." I believe we are each born with a voice. Instead of shoving each other out of the way in pursuit of our big solo, let's commit to building stages so that together we can take the platform and *sing*.

EIGHT

COMMIT TO COLLABORATION

Be a mountain, or lean on one.
Somali proverb

R EMEMBER THAT SEASON OF TUMULT I TOLD YOU about that followed our over-inventory disaster? While the conference call that
Travis and I hosted went a long way in confirming our commitment to
our partners—ambassadors and artisans alike—there were still plenty
of naysayers and plenty of trust needing to be rebuilt. Noonday's annual
ambassador conference, Shine, was the perfect place to cast vision and
rally commitment. But as I prepared for that year's message, my mind's
eye kept imagining the front row seats filled with my harshest critics. As
I was sharing my talk with one of my ambassador friends, she looked
me in the eyes and said, "Speak to those who believe deeply in our mission. Invest your time rallying those who want to be rallied, Jessica.
And let the naysayers fall away."

Her advice steadied me not only for that year's Shine Conference but
for many weeks beyond that event. "Rally those who want to be rallied"—
the sentiment stuck to me, mind and soul. *She's right,* I thought. At its
core, Noonday has always prided itself in being a powerful, mobilized

we. My job was to keep building upon this foundation by helping us to define the *we* I wanted us to be. We needed a proclamation of sorts, a set of reminders of who we are, a written rallying cry for those who wished to be rallied, a declaration: this is us.

To do that, we spent the following year working together with ambassadors and key people from our home office team to craft a manifesto, a statement that confirmed who this *we* truly is. When we unveiled that manifesto at Shine the following year, I realized how far we had come, how far *I* had come. I was no longer leading in fear. I was leading in confident faith. And crucially important, our community was committed. In many ways, this manifesto inspired this book because I believe it reaches far beyond Noonday. It has the power to embody us all.

The manifesto embodies my passion for building a collaborative culture at Noonday. I have seen this type of culture firsthand time and time again when I visit our artisan partners; this has given me the vision that it really is possible to create a reflexively collaborative culture.

On a recent trip to Uganda, I entered Jalia's living room to discover a regal, somewhat older woman garbed in traditional *kitenge* fabric. It was obvious from the moment I entered that this was an important visit. We were introduced, and then this woman and Jalia engaged in a lively discussion in Lugandan while sipping on passion fruit juice and tea. At one point, I saw the woman present a piece of paper that contained a long list, and before I knew it, Jalia was handing this woman what amounted to one hundred dollars in cash. Upon the woman's departure, I asked Jalia, "What on earth was that all about?"

Jalia explained that the woman was her former neighbor from the

NOONDAY COLLECTION AMBASSADOR MANIFESTO

We are a sisterhood—imperfectly courageous.

We believe in second tries and going scared.

When we look across the globe, we don't see strangers—we see ourselves.

Her dreams matter as much as mine.

So we don't judge; we do. We don't just talk; we act.

We believe that by styling our friends, we can change the world.

We are advocates in arm parties who style ourselves in authenticity and accessories, in confidence and clutches.

We apologize for our mistakes. We don't apologize for being ourselves.

We assume the best in each other.

By embracing our vulnerability, we create compassionate spaces of belonging for ourselves and others.

Her success doesn't diminish mine.

This is more than just jewelry; it's an invitation to join the journey.

We want nothing more than for women to stand up, step into their story, and own their worth.

We are better together.

We are Noonday Collection ambassadors.

village—the same woman who would check on Jalia and her siblings when they were young. Jalia's mother had found work in another village, which meant that Jalia and her siblings occupied a child-led house. They needed to be checked on, and this woman had filled that role.

"She is raising money for her daughter's wedding," Jalia explained, adding that in Uganda weddings are funded by the community—a few shillings from an aunt to pay for the cake, a few shillings from an old neighbor to hire the photographer, perhaps a few from a distant cousin to cover the napkins or the plates. I thought back to how embarrassed I felt regarding my neediness when hosting that first trunk show in my house and contrasted it with the decided *lack* of embarrassment I'd witnessed here. *Why do my friends and I always apologize for collaboration?* I wondered. *We have so very much to learn.*

Over the course of our friendship I've seen many examples of how Jalia has taken the collaborative culture of her childhood—one brought about by necessity in a polygamist family of forty children—and applied its best lessons to her business. Jalia's artisans are more than just coworkers; they are family to one another. They carry one another's burdens, celebrate one another's joys, and never hesitate to give of what they have when one of their family members is in need. Never was that collaborative culture more clearly at work than when Mama Jabal, one of the workshop's original members, found herself deprived of her every earthly possession.

You see, Mama Jabal had been in an abusive marriage for years with a man who treated her with about as much respect as he would a dog on the street. He not only abused her, but he also had multiple affairs and was involved with witchcraft. This man was a loose cannon, and one day he threw Mama Jabal and her two children out on the street with only the clothes on their backs. Suddenly, this strong and courageous woman found herself utterly destitute, with two kids to care for and no means to claim her rights.

Unfortunately, Mama Jabal is far from alone in her experience of abuse. In most of the world today, women continue to be oppressed, and in these places, violent conflict, extremist views, generations-long patriarchy, and abject poverty make for a wicked reality for women and girls, especially during times of war. Women and girls are targeted more than any other group by bigoted men with power. And women and girls suffer more than anyone else because of illiteracy, lack of proper medicine, lack of proper nutrition, lack of proper care during and after childbirth, and lack of adequate job opportunities.

Many of these women do not have a community that supports them. But thank God, Mama Jabal did. The day after her husband threw her out, Mama Jabal showed up for work at the workshop to find a spoon and a fork lying on her chair. Later that day, someone brought her a mosquito net. After lunch, bedsheets appeared at her worktable. Before she left work that day, Mama Jabal possessed the necessities that had been taken from her, as well as enough rent money to begin again. When you live in a collaborative culture, you ask for what you need and you give all that you can. As the Somali proverb says, you choose to either "be a mountain, or lean on one."

This collaborative way of life is on display in so many of the other communities we partner with too. Recently, my Ethiopian friend Cherry told me of five women who had left prostitution and entered the Women at Risk program, the program she founded to rescue women off the streets, which eventually morphed into the business that now makes some of our upcycled artillery pieces. Each of these women was pregnant with a daughter at the time. Cherry reflected on the many challenges they all had walked through during those years, saying that they'd known hills, valleys, victories, and defeats as together they navigated parenting, working, job loss, and just doing life as one. This is why it was such a blow to the group when one of the five women suffered a heart attack and died.

Cherry immediately assumed care of Tesfanish, the daughter of the deceased woman. But in actuality the community became the girl's mother. "A child belongs to us all," Cherry reflected. "We all pitched in to help." The other women talked with the girl, cooked meals for her, made clothes for her, and more. "They were a community of aunties," Cherry said, "who together served as mom."

A few years ago, all five of those daughters finished high school, passed their national exams, and left for university—a series of enormous accomplishments, all born of *going together* instead of alone.

Stories like these are powerful, and yet they can feel otherworldly to us. It's true: most likely, we will never experience crippling poverty, we will never be victims of brutal police crimes, and we will never know the harsh reality of being trafficked. But what we can all connect to is the idea that life often doesn't go at all like we expected it to and that things don't always turn out like we'd hoped. Regardless of where we live, where we've been, or what we've done, we *all* know how it feels to struggle and strain against a life we never asked for but suddenly find ourselves wading through. We *all* know how dark loneliness can feel. We *all* long for someone who will show up and speak up, telling us, "I'll share your struggle with you."

Around Noonday, we talk in terms of having a stakeholder model in which everyone involved in the business can flourish *at the same time.* This stakeholder approach is at the core of what it means for Noonday to be a certified B Corp (aka benefit corporation) and differs from the typical shareholder-only approach. Artisans, ambassadors, home office staff, trunk show hostesses, the bank that floats us our credit lines—we're all in this thing together, all pulling for the same goal. Jalia cares about the ambassador in Iowa, who feels pulled in a thousand directions as she raises four kids and books as many trunk shows as she can manage; and that same ambassador cares about the artisans on Jalia's team, who still struggle to pay for their kids' education. And something about that collaborative spirit makes each load seem more manageable.

Remember Wideleine, that tenacious woman who was forced by poverty to give up her daughter for adoption? Today, she is a living example of what collaboration can really do. Like many Haitians, Wideleine dreamed of one day owning her own plot of land with a sturdy house and a garden of her own. She knew it would be nearly impossible for her to meet this goal by herself, so rather than going it alone, she and a good friend from the workshop, Yvetta, decided to make their dreams a reality together. Because they had good jobs and reliable wages, they were able to set a little aside each month. They also received a land grant from the social-impact fund that their workshop runs today. Wideleine and Yvetta now share a plot of land that is all their own, have built modest but safe homes where they can raise their children, and have a sisterhood that is more precious than gold.

On a recent trip to Haiti, they wanted me to see their homes. Standing there, holding hands with the two of them, Yvetta on one side and Wideleine on the other, I couldn't help but think about the women who had held hands with me by first purchasing Noonday products and then by joining our ambassador team. This day was a culmination of collaboration that stretched from my backyard all the way across the globe.

One sure way to know that a culture has shifted toward collaboration is this: when a group of people come together to truly share the load, *division doesn't divide;* instead, it unifies.

This sounds impossible, I realize, but I'm living, breathing proof that it's true. And if you're part of a community of people whose *reflexive reaction* to relational tension is to launch an all-out seek-and-destroy mission for the sake of all parties involved, then you know that it's true as well. Division doesn't have to divide us; it can make us the strongest we've ever been.

Let me go back to that situation involving our excess inventory. What I didn't share with you before was that the artisan business leader who independently shared her fears and concerns with some ambassadors that led to a ripple effect of angst and uncertainty throughout the ambassador community was Jalia, the very woman I had partnered with since my first trunk show. My beloved friend Jalia and her artisan enterprise in Uganda were deeply impacted by our pendulum swing in order volume. It is easy to understand why she feared the future given the context of how difficult it was for her to lay off workers after seeing only explosive growth for several years in a row.

The fact that we're still as close as sisters today, and that we're still firing on all relational cylinders, is a testament to the compassionate, collaborative culture in which both of us reside. Yes, there may be a little drama along the way—*hello,* we're dealing with messy humans here—but resolution *can* come in the end.

The first time that I saw Jalia after that whole upheaval, we fell into each other's arms hugging more tightly than we'd ever hugged. During that period of several weeks, things had gotten pretty tense. I'd said things. She'd said things. But there we were, reunited, determined to sort everything out.

And if we had it to do all over again, she told me years later, she would have chosen trust over fear. "Me too," I said with a smile.

I picked up several lessons as I waded through that inventory ordeal, the main one centering on the importance of meaningful dialogue, which is essential if we are serious about creating a reflexively collaborative culture. Dialogue involves the free flow of meaning between two or more people and involves both *listening well* and *making generous assumptions,* even if generous assumptions aren't made about us. First, to the listening part of the equation.

Travis and I had many high-stakes conversations during that season with artisans, ambassadors, and with each other, and some of them, I really botched. In high-stakes conversations, two tendencies generally prevail. We either step into the proverbial boxing ring with bright red gloves, ready to uppercut our way to a win, or we sit glued to our ringside seats, refusing to engage at all. What I learned? There is another way. It takes intention, humility, curiosity, and practice, and it is essential for leading well. Instead of defending, indicting, and explaining (jab! hook! uppercut!), we can slip our hands out of our boxing gloves and make it our goal to create safety in the conversation instead. We can posture ourselves for empathy, for compassion, for peace, for love. And it is from this posture that the most miraculous things come out of our mouths. Things such as:

- "Tell me more."
- "I would love to understand your perspective more fully here."
- "Tell me what I can do better."
- "I have a lot to learn from you."
- "Is there more that you would like to share?"

Healthy dialogue isn't a boxing match at all; it's synchronized swimming—unified, others focused, graceful.

Second, meaningful dialogue must include making generous assumptions—in other words, giving people the benefit of the doubt. "Maybe that neighbor's decline on my dinner invitation wasn't really a rejection of me," we could tell ourselves. "Maybe that friend didn't call me back because her kid is sick, not because she doesn't care about me," we could say. "Maybe I am assigning meaning to that comment and it's actually not her intent."

Once I began to work on my communication skills, I saw that *my own assumptions* were often to blame for the conflict between other people and me. Give this a try. The next time you and another person conversationally bump into each other, take a deep breath and choose to believe the best rather than caving to the skepticism, cynicism, and insecurity that screams:

- *She's against me.*
- *She's mad at me.*
- *She hates me.*
- *She thinks I'm wrong.*
- *She meant to do it.*
- *She tried to harm me.*
- *She's out to get me.*
- *Things never work out for me.*

Regardless of how sticky the situation or how high the stakes seem, you and I are often only one conversation away from setting relational wrongs right. In truly collaborative cultures, disunity is chased down . . . *fast.* Instead of sitting and stewing, murmuring and gossiping, doubting and blaming, and all the rest, there is:

- generous assumption
- rational assessment
- clarifying conversation
- grace

In our community, we assume the best in each other, just like our ambassador manifesto says, and this positive intent is essential for a collaborative way of life.

Another way to tell that a collaborative spirit is taking root in and around you is that *anyone's joy is everyone's joy, and every success is owned by all.*

I told you before that I'm from San Antonio, famous for its Fiesta week and party culture. Accordingly, my wedding festivities included a ten-piece mariachi band, a live dancing band, a gourmet buffet, and about five hundred guests. During Joe's and my yearlong engagement, I had dreamed of all that our big day would entail, a common occurrence for any of us living in the resourced West. But in the developing world? Little girls there dream similar wedding-day dreams, and yet all too often, they never come true. Poverty can mean no food . . . no clean water . . . lack of proper medication, education, and work. But it can also mean no money to pay the legal fees required for a marriage certificate, which was the predicament faced by a Ugandan artisan named Bukenya, a proud member of Jalia's team.

Bukenya and his wife, Coral, had been committed to each other for years, and yet they could not afford the wedding certificate to make their marriage official. They worked for Jalia in her workshop crafting necklaces and other pieces for Noonday, and one day Jalia said to Bukenya, "You know, if you begin to save some of your pay, you could afford to have a wedding someday."

It took a full year for Bukenya to save the necessary funds, but in December 2012, Bukenya and Coral were married. But wait, it gets better still. There were so many couples in Bukenya and Coral's situation, couples who were finally working decent jobs and earning living wages but who still struggled to have any money left over for nonessentials, that the church decided to host a group wedding. This meant that the typical ceremonial fees could be divided across several couples—in this case, *nineteen* brides and grooms. Community members, family members, and beloved friends would donate money to a group wedding, and everyone would reap benefits as a result.

Bukenya sent me a picture of that wedding party, and it's an image I'll always treasure. Nineteen women in white standing tall and proud that day, their beaming new husbands at their sides. Even though the arrangement was born of necessity, I think those brides got the best of all possible worlds. There was something deeply poignant to me about those women banding together and sharing one of the most special and memorable days of their lives with one another. It was the spirit of collaboration that must have been swirling through that church. *Anyone's joy is everyone's joy. Every success is owned by all.*

———

Around Noonday, we are big on celebrating achievements regarding impact made, awards received, sales closed—basically, we love to *recognize.* But throughout the years, some ambassadors have challenged me, asking me how I can at once encourage them to set their own pace while simultaneously fist-bumping the woman who just hit five hundred thousand dollars in sales on stage at Shine.

The reason that I insist on acknowledging Noonday's top sellers and business leaders at our Shine Conference every year is not to diminish the contributions of everyone who is *not* standing on that stage, but rather to give every person sitting in that room tangible reasons to cheer. There is a healthy form of competition, and when we keep comparison rightly restrained, competition can be highly motivating. We can be competitive *and* collaborative—it's another way we can live an *and* existence in our *win/lose, either/or* world. Let me show you what I mean.

I participate in a boot-camp workout a few times a week here in Austin, and while the core class members are the same from session to session, there are others like me who pop in and out as they can. Group fitness always helps me work harder than I would work if I traipsed into the gym on my own, but I've noticed over this past year that when this woman named Julie shows up to class, I *kill it,* from the first rep to the last.

My guess is that Julie is about twenty-five years old, she is training for a triathlon, and she does not pee on herself while doing jumping jacks. I, on the other hand, am just trying to stay off anxiety meds, and evidently working out really helps with that. But what I find is that whenever Julie is there, I work harder. I move faster. I focus more intently on the muscles I'm asking to move. It's not being tethered to Julie in a PE-class sort of way. There is no dragging of Jessica across a field. There is just solid encouragement from an example of someone who is powerful and persistent and *ripped.* Because she keeps going for the entire sixty minutes of class, I keep going. Because she pushes past her comfort zone, I push past my comfort zone too. Because she gives every-thing she's got, I give what I have too. Not so that I can earn my worth via those efforts but so that I can *join her* in health and wellness. The competition that I engage in isn't perfect-non-peeing-triathlete Julie versus me, the opposite of all that. No, no: the competition is *me versus me,* me versus my best on that day. Julie is simply my pacing partner for sixty rock-star-Jessica minutes.

I'm telling you, if you will let this idea seep into your soul, you can line your wall with trophies and enjoy countless victory celebrations, while not staking an ounce of your identity on any of it. No more an-gling for position. No more posturing to impress the people around you. No more lusting after someone else's lifestyle. We can be people who choose to let others' joy bubble up inside us too.

Another telltale sign that collaboration is becoming your norm is this: the process of asking one another for help, for partnership, or for com-pany is as automatic as wanting coffee first thing in the morning.

My friend Mica, a fellow entrepreneur, loves to share a story about her first-grade self. One afternoon, Mica picked up the phone and started calling friends to see if anyone could come over to play. "Hey, can you come over?" Mica said to the first girl, who said, "No. Sorry, I can't." No problem. Mica would just ask someone else . . . but wouldn't you know it, that girl also declined, as well as the girl after that.

Unbeknownst to Mica, her mom was listening in on these calls. After the third decline, Mica's mom was compelled to rush to her daughter's aid, to shield her from rejection and pain. But just as she was taking steps toward Mica, she noticed that Mica had picked up the phone yet again. "Oh, that's okay," Mica said to friend number four. "Maybe next time! Bye!"

"I don't know what stopped my mom from rescuing me," present-day Mica will tell you, "but for some reason, she stayed away. Evidently, I called a full *ten* girlfriends before I found a single one who could play."

Upon finding that available playmate, Mica hung up the phone, rounded the corner, and announced to her mom, "Good news! Valerie can come over to play!"

I love this story because it beautifully demonstrates what it means to be an asker, to keep inviting people in, regardless of who says yes and who says no. When we live in a collaborative culture, asking loses its worrisome quality and becomes something that feels completely natural. When we are living in the give-and-take, no one keeps a running tally of favors requested or bestowed. There's no fear of imposing or looking selfish, because it is understood that *together* is what we are. We believe that we can't do it alone, and so we become free to be askers who make their needs known without shame. After that first Noonday trunk show—when I feared that no one would show—I gained confidence in "the ask." Eventually, when guests at trunk shows told me that they had a friend or relative who might be interested in hosting a show of her own, I boldly asked for that person's name and number, and then I followed up the next day.

Often these women lived in other towns, and so I would load up my jewelry samples, bags, and displays and haul them to Houston or San Antonio or Dallas. But because we were still on the financial-struggle bus, I couldn't afford to stay in a hotel during my visit. Not only did I ask these women to open their homes to trunk shows, then, but also to an overnight guest.

Are you recoiling in horror at the thought of asking a stranger if you can crash at her place? It's true: perhaps you won't find yourself in this exact "ask" on your journey toward intention and impact. But I guarantee you, you will find yourself in situations where the path forward is paved by boldly asking for what you need. If you've got a go-getting spirit stirring within you, then you'll be led collaboration's way. But nobody will be there to help you, unless you muster the nerve to ask.

Whatever "ask" your dream is pushing you to make, I encourage you to take this same attitude. If you believe in what you're hustling for, then let your passion come out in your words. Don't keep it all to yourself. Invite others to join you in this beautiful thing you're building. People long to be needed, to contribute. When we ask of someone, we say to her, "You have value and something to offer. I'd be honored if you'd join me in this." I believe that is one of the most empowering messages you can send. When asking simply becomes reflexive, we all benefit and our community becomes stronger than we could have ever imagined.

The final indicator that your community is truly embracing a spirit of collaboration is that goodbyes are never forever and endings become just as important as beginnings. When we have recognized our need for one another, it becomes nearly impossible to simply say goodbye and walk away—which is good, because I hate goodbyes. Sure, the dynamics shift here and there, but do things really need to end?

You probably would acknowledge the importance of making a good first impression, but have you ever stopped to consider the *last impression* you make? Noonday's former VP of product accepted a role with another organization and now lives and works in New York. But

whenever Noonday launches a new collection, she sends me a congratulatory text. Our partnership never ended—it just looks different now.
The "ending" was only the start of something new.

If you want to grow in your career, then you'll do well to adopt this
approach. Never slam a door shut. Keep those relationships alive. Because you never know when an opportunity to collaborate again will
present itself, and those opportunities have the potential to springboard
you to where you want to be. After all, if I hadn't doggedly kept in
touch with my college friend Laura, I never would have gone to visit her
in Uganda. And it was on that trip that I reconnected with Downie and
was handed the opportunity to sell boxes of beautiful Ugandan jewelry
to fund raise for my adoption.

On our final night in-country on a recent trip to Haiti, ambassadors
and artisans alike had gathered on the beach to share our most memorable moments from the week. It was then someone suggested that we
take a group photo so that we could seal this experience of connection
and togetherness for all time. It was dusk, and the sunset was gorgeous.
Without really planning on it, as soon as the guy who agreed to snap
the photo was set, all ten women jumped into the air. Because our photographer was shooting into the setting sun, the ocean at our backs, all
that turned out in the final photo is the ten of us silhouetted against sky
and sand. But honestly? I think it's better that way. I kind of like that
our faces are obscured. Because in this version, our real significance isn't
in our individuality but in our togetherness as we take our big leap.

That's how it goes with collaborative cultures, you know? Either
we're in this thing together, or else we aren't in it at all.

PART THREE

A WORLD
CHANGED

NINE

WIDEN YOUR CIRCLE

When we look across the globe, we
don't see strangers—we see ourselves.
Noonday Collection Ambassador Manifesto

I N THE PREVIOUS CHAPTER, WE LOOKED AT THE importance of building a collaborative culture in your life—one that celebrates similari-
ties and turns differences into opportunities to grow. In this section, I'm
asking you to widen the circle of acceptance and compassion that makes
it possible for others to flourish. Stretch it out until it covers your community, your state, your country. Then, keep stretching until the *whole
world* is encased.

Yes, I'm asking you to invite the whole world into your circle of
empathy. Sound overwhelming? It is, unless your attempts are anchored
in genuine human connection. The fact is, we can read news story after
news story about the Syrian refugee crisis, we can share a Facebook post
about child trafficking, and we can drop off canned food at the local
food bank, but unless we allow those noble efforts to connect us to real
live people, we won't get very far. Ultimately, courage is ignited through
connection, and connection happens only when eyes and souls meet.
Infants develop as their parents gaze lovingly into their eyes. Children

mature by learning to make eye contact. And adults, it turns out, finally risk changing the world in which they live by seeing—*really seeing*—one another.

———————

One of the best and worst days of my life is the day I resuscitated my son, Holden, from a near-drowning incident. Amelie, Holden, and I had met up with four moms and their children at a neighborhood pool. Once the other moms and I had settled the little kids far away from the water to eat lunch, I told my friends that I was going to jump into the water with the big kids. Amelie jumped to me first, and just as I caught her, I happened to glance over my shoulder, something having caught my eye. That's when I saw my two-year-old floating on the water's surface, facedown.

I flew through the water that now felt like quicksand to get to my son and swam to the pool's side, Holden's limp body in my arms. I hoisted him out of the pool, onto the blazing-hot concrete, and began pumping his heart with my palms, screaming to Jesus while recalling my last high school CPR class. After what felt like an eternity, Holden's purple lips spat out pool water, and his blue face regained its flesh tone. Even though my friends had already dialed 911, I ran to my car, loaded Holden up, and sped to the ER. A kind nurse took my insurance card and my driver's license and then ushered me toward an exam area, where my boy and I waited for an X-ray tech to come take Holden's scans, to ensure there was no further water in his lungs. We still have the stuffed animal the nurse handed him that day.

Hours later, I arrived home with Holden, my boy safe and my heart grateful, even as I was shaken to my core.

Sometime after that accident had come and gone, I reflected on the resources that had facilitated Holden's rescue that day: a CPR class, a 911 call, an available car, a fully equipped emergency room, a health insurance process that worked for me . . . Each of these tools is quite useful, wouldn't you agree, in the face of real crisis, whenever it hits?

A year later, I was out shopping when I received a call from Jalia. "Jessica," Jalia said, her voice urgent and clipped. "We're in an emergency here. I need to find help for Mama Sham."

Within moments, I had the full context of what had happened. Mama Sham, one of Jalia's artisans in Uganda, had awakened two weeks prior to discover that her body was completely paralyzed. Since she had previously been in an abusive marriage for years and was now living as a single mother, her kids had stepped up to become her caretakers. For fourteen days, then, Mama Sham had relied on her four children to lift her body when she needed to move, change her clothes when the old ones were soiled, put food into her mouth when she was hungry, and lay her down when it was time to sleep.

As I listened to the fear in Jalia's voice, my thoughts raced back to my own experience with Holden, when death had looked our family straight in the eye and, by the grace of God, had blinked. My son had returned to me healthy and safe, but had he been born in many other places in the world, that would likely not have been the case. That momentary vulnerability had woken me up to the painfully persistent vulnerability of people living in the developing world—and in a way that reading about it in the newspaper or watching a documentary never could have.

For Mama Sham, the reality of that vulnerability was hitting her family and friends with a vengeance. In Uganda, there is no *dialing 911*. There is no *hopping in your car to head to the ER*. There is no *on-call*

X-ray tech, eager to help. Sure, Mama Sham's children could have called for an ambulance, but that would have required cash—in hand—upon arrival. Once at the hospital, still more cash would have been required of Mama Sham to receive even a moment of the doctor's time. Mama Sham did not have cash on hand, and so she lay in her home, certain that there she would die.

"Jessica," Jalia said to me, "we have to help our friend. We can't let her live this way."

The question here wasn't *whether* Noonday would help. The question before us was *how.*

———

You and I both know that things in our world are wrong and that we have a part to play in setting them right. However, all too often, we respond by keeping suffering at arm's length, choosing to live with a low-grade guilt instead of engaging. We often keep our circle of compassion small because we are afraid that once we are aware of the needs of the wider circle, we'll have to take responsibility for fixing the problem and sacrifice our comfort in the process. We are afraid that we will say the wrong thing, do the wrong thing, or give to the wrong cause in our attempts to make things better. Or, we are afraid that waking up to the suffering of others will send us spiraling, unable to cope with the emotional weight.

Now, lest you think that I'm just some bleeding heart who reads *Half the Sky* for fun and spends every weekend marching, who signs all the petitions that come through her inbox, or who clicks on every opportunity to support a cause on Facebook, let me set the record straight: I'm not. But increasingly, I want to be. As it turns out, founding a fair-trade company is not an antidote for my own human tendency to prioritize my own comfort over action. I am the person who flips to the end of a book just to brace myself for the disappointment and grief headed my way. I am one of those cynical ones who wonders about the efficacy of many of the fund-raising campaigns that I receive. And you will not find a slew of heartbreaking but important documentaries in my Netflix queue (I prefer heart-racing suspense). Most painful to admit, when my attorney friend Norbert gifted me with a book titled *The Men Who Killed Me: Rwandan Survivors of Sexual Violence,* I placed it on my shelf and never cracked the spine because I didn't want to carry the burden of the sadness I knew those pages bore. I do, however, continue to grow in my ability to expand my circle of compassion, and fortunately my journey has only just begun.

My point in telling you these rather humbling confessions is this: you don't need to achieve perfection as you expand your circle of compassion to draw near to suffering. *You simply need to draw near.* Because when we truly connect with people, it becomes much more difficult to prioritize our comfort over their clear and present needs. If I had simply read about Mama Sham's condition on somebody's Facebook wall, I would have felt sympathy for her, to be sure. But I can't say that that sympathy would have spurred me to *empathy.* Sympathy says, "I feel sorry for you," while empathy says, "I could have been you." When I got that phone call from Jalia, though, Mama Sham's plight was instantly real to me. I knew her. She was my friend. I empathized with her and was compelled to help. And help, we did: in a matter of hours, Noonday had funded every penny of Mama Sham's five-thousand-dollar surgery.

Empathy is what makes it possible for us to move when we feel like standing still. And empathy comes only when we break down our walls and invite someone into our newly expanded circle.

I first woke up to the grave injustices that exist in our world when I was a teenager, and man, did my youthfulness show. I often tripped over my big mouth and my even bigger earrings in my attempt to love well. I handed out lollipops and American books to kids who could not read English, for instance. I told a little girl I met in Kenya that I would sponsor her forever but soon failed to keep in touch. I stood on a soapbox pointing a finger at my peers to care for the poor when they were just trying to make it through cheerleading tryouts.

In my own defense, I had but two global experiences under my belt, and while my efforts toward doing something to help were imperfect and ill informed, something was better than nothing, I figured . . . Surely, I'd get better at this as I went. And so I went, and went, and went.

During the summer following my freshman year of college, I interned with the Church of the Savior in Washington, DC, at Samaritan Inns, the home that served women coming from twenty-eight-day detox facilities. Looking back, I want to take into my hands the young, tender face of the teenage version of me and give it a precious little squeeze over some of the responses I gave to the women with whom I lived. My job as an intern meant stocking the pantry with items from the food bank, opening the locked door for women as they came and left for job interviews, and attending Narcotics Anonymous meetings with the women. One day, during a house meeting with all the residents, we discussed some tensions brewing in the house. After asking one resident, Wanda, what bothered her, she pointed at me and said, "I will *tell* you what my problem is. My problem is *her*. I ain't *nobody's* summer project."

I froze. I saw the scene as though it were playing on a movie screen—young, white-privileged know-it-all, tending to my daily to-dos with cheerfulness to spare, sitting there in a circle surrounded by women who had more grit in their pinky fingers than this girl possessed in her entire frame. I would have spared everyone some misery back then if I had already learned to value listening and making generous assumptions. In a moment that necessitated my listening well, I instead boiled over in defense: "No one is my summer project, except maybe *Jesus*. I can't help but feel like I'm being blamed for something here."

Perhaps "Tell me more about that, Wanda" would have been a more productive path to take.

Later that week, I apologized to Wanda for not listening to her or being open to her point of view. She graciously received my apology, letting me know that it had been hard for her to be around a girl my age who seemingly had it together because, when she was my age, she had been living on the streets. She invited me to visit her the following week at work, where she served lunch at Whole Foods. As she handed me my order that day, I thanked her for giving me a second chance at being her friend.

The lesson I took away from that season with Wanda is that people are made to be loved, not fixed. People are not problems to be solved. Far better is banishing the *us versus them* and seeing all people as part of ourselves. We don't feel sorry for people; we see ourselves in people. And as a result, we expand our circles of compassion to include not just us, not just people who look like us, but *all people.*

We *all* bear the image of a perfect God, and thus we all deserve life reflective of the dignity that we bear.

I made my first big move after college to Latin America with the organization Food for the Hungry. Before leaving for the field, my forty new
comrades and I went through an intensive training led by Steve Cor-
bett. Steve would go on to work for the Chalmers Center for Economic
Development and then write the book *When Helping Hurts,* about the
unintended consequences associated with Western aid.

But for now Steve was simply our guide at a rigorous month-long
camp in Arizona aimed at baptizing the lot of us in the world of community development and cross-cultural living.

So much of what I learned during that time put my previous experiences into a context that developed into a worldview of sorts. Steve explained that often when the privileged try to help the poor, we do so with
the perspective of wanting to make them more like us—in a phrase,
materially rich. We summarize poverty into one issue, boiling it down
to a simple lack of physical resources. But giving well-intended hand-
outs can lead to a vicious cycle, increasing the pride of the giver and the
dependency of the recipient, without ever addressing poverty's roots.

Steve painted a broader picture of the activist Jesus, the One I'd
encountered during my youth in food banks and treatment facilities.
He explained that God is a relational God and that since human be-
ings are created in the image of God, we are relationally wired as well,
wired to relate to God, self, others, and the rest of creation. Providing
material goods, while important, is not the sole solution to poverty.
Helping the poor is not about making them more like us, it turns out;
it is about helping them live out their own authentic selves as image
bearers of God. It's about creating a space for humans to express their
humanness.

It was a perfect way to put into context what I had experienced in
my teens in Kenya, DC, and in my own backyard—that human be-

ings, no matter where they live, deserve to feel human. Humanness is getting sung to on your eighth birthday by a mom who doesn't have to be concerned about whether you'll have food to eat that day. Humanness is receiving a proper paycheck upon completing a job. Humanness is being able to count on the police for protection. It is being able to sleep under the same roof as your child. But the truth is, millions of people around the world are not experiencing basic humanness.

Subhuman living looks like the poor having little influence to defend themselves against injustice, which means that the powerful can commit acts of violence against them with impunity.

Subhuman living looks like people who have HIV being viewed as pariahs in their communities, despite the condition's being every bit as treatable as type 2 diabetes. Throughout my trips to Ethiopia, I've met many women whose HIV status caused their families to disown them, making them even more vulnerable to exploitation and abuse. Without the safety net of a supportive community, then, the disease *is* a sentence to death.

Subhuman living looks like gender-based discrimination, one of the most crippling cultural norms that still exists. One of Noonday's partners in India, a woman named Moon, shared with me that her birth was welcomed with tears of sadness and disappointment, "because I was born a girl instead of a boy. My mother, my grandmother, and my other family members received me as a burden . . . a perception I couldn't help believing was true."

Moon would face discrimination every day of her life, and yet she finally was able to complete her education, begin working as a leader with our artisan venture, and chart a new course for her life. But those early days left a real mark on her. "I still fight," Moon recently told me. "Every day, I fight."

If our goal is to elevate the dignity of human worth, then our approach to work must support that goal.

Following the training with Food for the Hungry, I moved to one of the most beautiful and remote areas of the Bolivian Andes and experienced rural living for the first time. While living in these small Quechuan communities, I began noticing a common denominator among those who were freed from poverty's grip: they all possessed a spirit of *entrepreneurship,* what Harvard Business School professor Howard Stevenson defines as "the pursuit of opportunity beyond resources controlled."[1] Entrepreneurship is that tendency to make something from nothing, that unsinkable propensity to not only see potential but also *act* on the potential you've seen. Case in point: Sinforesa, who weaved by day and sold crackers and Coca-Cola from her home's storefront at night. We would guzzle down those Cokes hot, with no ice, but truly, we didn't care. That familiar taste worked wonders on our homesick hearts, and we got to support Sinforesa's venture—a win-win situation, my friends and I agreed.

By contrast, I also witnessed firsthand some of the unintended consequences of well-meaning Western aid. While hiking through the majestic Andes, I occasionally came upon an adobe structure filled with recently harvested potatoes, the result of a well-meaning NGO assessment that yielded the building of scores of these latrines. The problem was that the NGO never consulted a single member of the community about this supposed need of theirs, and nobody in the village *cared about having latrines.* And so the villagers accepted the latrines that they neither wanted nor planned to use and promptly converted them to storage closets—expensive ones, at that.

I began to think about my well-intentioned past with Wanda, the people who were homeless that I'd worked with during college, and many others. Had I ever stopped to see life through their eyes? Or in my rush to do good, had I simply projected my own solutions onto them? Maybe Wanda had been right. Projectizing people is *exactly* what I had done.

I ended up eventually moving to Guatemala to be near Joe, and the shift provided a perfect opportunity to gain a new perspective on the value and importance of work. In Guatemala, I tried to be more curious—to listen more, to notice *need* from a fresh point of view.

In Guatemala, as I got to know the families in our community and the families of the children I taught, I saw the value of entrepreneurship. It wasn't just that offering people a business opportunity was a way to help people out of poverty; in my increasingly informed view, it was the *best* way to help them, while still honoring their intrinsic abilities and dignity. Granted, while there was nothing inherently wrong with Westerners' proud propensity for refusing little luxuries and sending money to Kenya (hadn't I initially done this very thing?), there was a more effective means for securing livelihood. In the same way that giving a woman a fish helps her for only that day, the few dollars I'd sent over could go only so far. A better approach would have been finding a way to teach that woman to fish, a solution that could help her not for a day but for a lifetime. Even better still? Helping that woman open a fish shop, a solution that could positively influence not only her own life but also the lives of her kids and their kids, for generations to come.

The first time I'd heard of a business being able to fuel real social change was during a guest talk at the University of Texas. Ben Cohen and Jerry Greenfield, founders of Ben & Jerry's ice cream, were on campus, and a friend invited me to come along to hear them speak. While I am sure the pair spoke brilliantly and eloquently about how they innovated their delicious Chubby Hubby and Cherry Garcia flavor offerings, my big takeaway from hearing their talk was a single comment they made: "Educational institutions and charities are not the most powerful force in modern society. *Business* is that force. It is the *greatest force for good* in the world."[2]

I later learned that Ben & Jerry's was one of the first companies in history to position a social mission as equally important to its product-based and economic missions. They eventually helped unify and start the benefit corporation (B Corp) and became one of the first companies to gain B Corp certification. Perhaps the resonance I felt with the concept was a foreshadowing of sorts; today Noonday Collection is a Certified B Corp that uses business as a force for good.

Through my time living overseas, I concluded that the motivation for my work would be to empower others to experience their full humanness and dignity. I think of the Kenyan woman enthusiastically arranging fruit to sell at her fruit stand and Wanda proudly serving customers in her apron that bore the name Whole Foods, and I see a beautiful image of how work acknowledges the dignity intrinsic to our own human worth. And no matter where I go in the world, I see this universal truth: *people are longing for good jobs.* In fact, Gallup's World Poll "across 160 countries found that over the last 100 years the great global dream has changed from wanting peace, freedom and family to simply wanting to have a good job."[3] What the world wants most? Dignified work.

Over the years, people have asked me to comment on what sets Noonday apart from other direct-sales companies, other social entrepreneurships, and other fashion businesses, and my answer still energizes me today: We always believe in linked prosperity, which simply means that all stakeholders connected to our business should thrive as we thrive. From the artisans with whom we partner, who hand make every piece we sell, to the ambassadors who promote the products, to the employees at our Austin home office who keep everything running well, we are an interdependent network of stakeholders who each have something to offer. We are connected. We are allies. The sum of our work is greater than each part; together we rise or we fall.

With our emphasis on interconnectivity, then, we gauge our bottom-line success according to meaningful opportunities for artisans and ambassadors created around the world instead of measuring it only in dollars and cents. So, while yes, we are a direct-sales social-impact fashion brand, we are first an opportunity machine. We believe that to have the greatest impact, and for us to empower people at the highest level, we must invite those who are living in under-resourced conditions to experience not the fleeting delight of a handout but rather the sustainable dignity of *work*.

Like Ben and Jerry, I am convinced that when business is done right, it honors the innate human dignity in every person involved in the enterprise. Whereas so much of development has historically been about lending aid, Noonday's approach is about harnessing the talents and abilities of people living in vulnerable communities, to help them pull themselves out of poverty while simultaneously creating opportunity for female entrepreneurs here in the United States. Social entrepreneurship is about recognizing that every person, poor or rich, educated or not, privileged or disenfranchised, has something valuable to offer and something to bring to the table.

Contrary to popular perception, entrepreneurship isn't limited to venture-capital funding, spreadsheets, MBAs, and looking the part of a traditional businesswoman; it's about taking the resources you've got, no matter how limited they may be, and transforming them into something new, something that's more than the sum of its parts.

———————

When I think of these two world-changing acts—widening your circle and harnessing business to create change—one woman leaps to mind. Rosario is a petite Guatemalan woman with killer dimples and a kind heart who leads the artisan business that produces some of Noonday's beloved hand-beaded accessories. It's always a joy to visit Rosario in her village near Lake Atitlán in the Guatemalan highlands. On a recent trip we met in the home of one of her employees, a woman named Alicia. As the three of us perched ourselves on her bed, Alicia began to share with me how Rosario has impacted her life.

"Five years ago," Alicia told me, "I had none of what you see now. My life was very hard." She went on to explain that because her mother, who is diabetic, needed help affording the life-saving medication she required, Alicia was forced to drop out of school as a teenager to find work. Work was hard to find, though, and the family found themselves struggling to survive.

Next door, Rosario and her family had fallen on difficult economic times too. Rosario's father owned an artisan business of his own, but orders had slowed to a near halt. Even so, when Rosario and her family saw how much Alicia and her family were struggling, they immediately committed to helping. "You're like family to us," she told Alicia. "We're going to find a way to create work for you." Although she would have been totally justified in focusing on her own well-being during this time, Rosario didn't hesitate to widen her circle to embrace Alicia and her family. She committed to collaboration and determined that she would find a way to change her friend's situation.

Rosario's family taught Alicia how to bead and hired her to create artisan crafts with them. To afford Alicia's first paycheck, they all pooled their money—Rosario, her brothers, and her dad—to make sure Alicia could buy the medication her mother needed.

It was about this time that I got connected with Rosario and saw the beautiful pieces she and her team were creating. Noonday began placing regular orders with the business, and soon things began to change for Rosario's family and Alicia's family alike. But it wouldn't have happened if Rosario hadn't widened her circle of compassion and committed to using her business to pull Alicia out of poverty along with her.

Today, Alicia is married, and she and her husband are expecting their first child. As we sat on the bed in Alicia's home, I asked if I could pray for her and her baby. I put my hand on her baby bump, and tears welled up in my eyes. Because that child's mama has a dignified job as a jewelry maker, the little one in Alicia's womb will not have to quit school to support a family. This child will be able to go to school and flourish. *This* is why we do what we do.

If we are going to live for something bigger than ourselves in this world, it's essential that we widen our circles to include not just ourselves, not just our neighbors, but people around the world. But to widen those circles, we have to be able to recognize the needs of this world. And to do that we've got to shake off our slumber and finally wake up to the needs of those around us. You see, waking up is what happens when we *really see* this world and we show up with consciousness we didn't once possess. We wake up to the realities all around us; we wake up to the way things really are; we wake up to our own power, now set in context; we get woke, and we're never again the same.

What is the step that *you* need to take in waking up to life beyond yourself? What fears and self-protective tendencies are preventing you from deeply connecting with the suffering of others and finding the fuel you need to do something about it? What book can you read (I'm glad you're here), what person can you invite into your life whose background is different from yours, what community meeting can you attend, or what conversation can you begin?

The world needs your contribution, even if that contribution feels awfully small right now. I believe that each of us has a responsibility to use what we have been given—and believe me, girl, you have been given a lot—to build a flourishing world. When we take the risk to erase the lines we have drawn around ourselves that keep us comfortable and we pitch our tent in the great unknown, viewing others as extensions of us, we'll realize something incredible. The solution to the problems we see? It's not others. It's *us*.

TEN

LEVERAGE YOUR POWER

The place God calls you to is the
place where your deep gladness
and the world's deep hunger meet.

Frederick Buechner

I F YOU'VE BEEN FEELING LIKE LIFE IS A GAME of freeze tag and you
have been in the frozen position way too long, then allow me to tag
you. You are it! As International Justice Mission founder Gary Haugen
said, "God has a plan to help bring justice to the world—and his plan
is us."[1] You and I are free to stand up, to speak up, and to affect this
world in need. And isn't that our endgame here? Think about it: Why
bother waking up to the realities of injustice, unless we're going to *act*
on that state of wakefulness . . . unless we will commit to effecting
change?

Over the years, I've found that once a woman begins to rip off
the layers of bubble wrap that have kept her isolated and insulated and
she experiences the exhilaration of living life as it was meant to be lived,
the bubble wrap tube gets put back on the shelf, next to the scissors and

packing tape. Even a passing glance at those tiny plastic pouches makes her cringe.

Once she gets a taste—even a tiny taste—of this life-beyond-ourselves reality, she can't help but hunger for more. The question then becomes, *What do I do about it?*

––––––––

By way of answering that question, I will refrain from telling you to follow in my footsteps because, as you'll recall, those twists and turns would probably give you vertigo. I went here and there and everywhere in search of my "calling," proving that this process is anything but a perfectly straight line, where one point leads predictably to the next. And while I don't begrudge any of the wild experiences I've had along the way, for the simple fact that each of them taught me something I didn't yet know, I wish I'd been able to embrace my own unique journey and avoid the bait of a you-*should*-do-this sort of life.

If you want to show solidarity with the poor, Jessica, I told myself, *then you* should *quit wearing makeup, carrying a designer bag, and spending any money* at all.

If you want to make a real difference, Jessica, then you should *get a social work degree.*

If you want to serve people in need, Jessica, then you should *become a teacher.* (Listen, while I love my kids, I don't necessarily love yours. Let's just say my master's degree in education has been better left unutilized.)

Many years ago, I followed a blog written by an eighteen-year-old named Katie Davis who moved to Uganda and subsequently adopted thirteen girls by the time she was twenty-three. I remember feeling a pang of guilt: *She's a teenager and has already done all this?* my insecure ego would prod me. *What have you done today to make a difference, recycled your kombucha bottle?*

The fact is, each of us is distinctly wired and has unique skills and interests to bring to bear on making this world a better place. To paste anyone's journey on top of my own and assume that my path should look like hers is an ill-fated strategy for finding the life that I, alone, was made to live. The truth is, those things that make our hearts beat a little faster with excitement are not random. They are distinctly—perhaps even *divinely*—placed.

No matter how different our gifts may appear, it's true that each of us has something unique to bring to the table. An example of this from my personal life came in the form of a resilient Rwandan teenager named Rachel. Rachel came into my life after I received a text from my friend Natalie, who works for a Rwandan organization called Africa New Life. Among other things, Africa New Life provides medical evacuation and care for the most extreme medical cases in Rwanda; Natalie was reaching out to me because Rachel needed help.

Specifically, Rachel needed an Austin-based foster family to care for her before and after the intensive brain surgery she required. Natalie asked me, Did I know anyone who might be interested? It was only for six months—*maybe* a year.

When I heard about Rachel's situation, my thoughts chased to Dee, one of my close friends and a nurse who happened to live near the hospital where Rachel would have her surgery performed. Now, Dee was already a busy mom of three, living with her husband in a cozy urban home with no guest bedroom and few resources to spare. But that didn't stop Dee and Tim from saying a hearty yes to taking in this girl whom they'd never met.

Dee and Tim ended up fostering Rachel for more than a year and a half, during which time Dee served as Rachel's personal nurse, foster mother, and friend. During Rachel's intense but successful surgery, Dee spent every night in the hospital by her side, just as she would have done for her own children. And afterward, when Rachel was unable to care for herself in the most basic of ways, Dee bathed her, bandaged her wounds, and nursed her back to full health.

During those months, my Noonday travel schedule had me out of town far more often than in, and as our Austin community rallied around the family, I became painfully aware that I wasn't pitching in like our other friends, such as by helping to pick up Rachel from school or tutoring her in ESL. As I watched my community rally around Dee's needs, I began to wonder what exactly I had to offer.

One day, I ran by Trader Joe's for my family's groceries and realized that just because I couldn't help in the same ways that my friends were, there was still *something* that I could do. I loaded up my cart with cookie butter and chocolate-covered almonds, neither of which Dee and Tim would buy for themselves, as well as all the makings for that night's dinner, and I dropped off bags of groceries at their home, mere blocks from mine. And then I just kept doing it, week after week after week.

In the end, people from all walks of life and with varied giftings, strengths, and scheduling margin offered what they could, and in so doing lifted up an entire family.

————————

Dee's story is important for us to consider because it reminds us that while we can't do *all* the things, and while our souls would never forgive us for doing *none* of the things, there are only *certain* things that are ours to do. And so, before you saddle yourself with all manner of paralyzing expectations—"Gosh, now that I know my power, I guess I need to start my own socially conscious business, adopt thirteen children, replace my non-fair-trade clothes with thrift-store finds, and sell all my earthly possessions so that I can route those profits to the poor"—please know that this is not what I'm asking of you. I'm not asking you to be Katie Davis, or anyone else for that matter. I'm just asking you to be *you*, awake and living with impact, exactly where you are.

If entrepreneurship is in your heart, like it has always been for me, then you might choose to make a difference in the world by embarking on a journey of "conscious capitalism," a term coined by Whole Foods' John Mackey to describe businesses that seek to make an impact in addition to making a profit. Part of my goal with Noonday Collection has been to help reshape perceptions about how we alleviate poverty. While developmental aid has its purpose, we simply can't overstate the potential of entrepreneurship as a means for transforming communities in a sustainable and dignified way. The conscious-capitalism credo asserts that "business is good because it creates value, it is ethical because it is based on voluntary exchange, it is noble because it can elevate our existence, and it is heroic because it lifts people out of poverty and creates prosperity."[2] So, if you've got a passion for multiplying your resources, creating empowering work for others, and growing something that lasts, conscious capitalism might be just the framework for you.

And don't feel like you need to run off and start something! Think about how you can apply this framework to what you are already doing. If you're a Realtor, then this might mean using your business to help someone who is traditionally left out of the home-buying process. If you're a photographer, then it might mean photographing teens who can't afford senior portraits or volunteering to take photos for a Heart Gallery that helps children available for adoption in the United States to find homes. If you're an accountant, then it could mean lending your services free of charge to an organization you believe in, so that they can get their books in order. No matter what career or life path you're traveling, there is an opportunity with your name on it, to harness your gifts and abilities to make a difference in other people's lives.

Or it could mean taking on something completely outside your realm of work, to dive in to something you're passionate about. When Noonday's in-house writer, Jenna, began to learn about the brokenness of our country's foster-care system, she knew that she needed to get involved somehow. Her one-bedroom apartment didn't lend itself well to foster parenting, but there were no such housing considerations for becoming a CASA volunteer. Volunteering with CASA—Court Appointed Special Advocates—allows her to speak up for children who have been abused or neglected while bridging the gap between the many people involved in a Child Protective Services case to ensure the children's best interests are represented. Rather than allowing her limitations to define her involvement, Jenna kept searching for another way to make a difference. I encourage you to do the same.

Over the years, I've engaged in countless discussions with other women, wrestling with what it means to live awake and how to apply their unique passions, skills, and resources to meeting the needs of others, and I've noticed an interesting trend. Almost without exception, the highest-impact investments those women have been able to make were catalyzed by pushing on one of five aspects of life. Beyond simply reading a book, watching a documentary, finishing a 5K, or writing a check, the steps of faith that were catalyzed in these women's lives whenever they recalibrated one or more of these five things are what led them to going all in with this beyond-ourselves sort of life. Let me give them to you here, before we dive in further together. They are:

1. My Power
2. My Pocketbook
3. My Priorities
4. My Proximity
5. My Perspective

If you're looking for an on-ramp to take you from anecdotal impact to impact as a lifestyle, then I bet you'll find it somewhere in this list. Ready to see if I'm right?

1. My Power: What if I used my power to fuel not only my own life but the lives of others too?

I hesitated to share many stories about my upbringing in this book for fear that I would come off as a pouty, impetuous, poor-pitiful-me product of white privilege. It's true: I could add #FirstWorldProblems to a lot of the narratives in my life. But even though I can't change where I was born or to what family, something important I've learned is that I still can effect positive change.

Listen, if you were born in the resourced West and have light-colored skin, then you need to reconcile a certain amount of privilege in your life just like me. But instead of letting that privilege guilt you into paralysis, sort out how to invest it for good. If we've got it, I say, then let's look it in the eye, gather it up, and give it away.

Maybe that description doesn't fit you at all. Maybe you've faced your own fair share of prejudice or poverty or disempowerment. But no matter how the world has attempted to silence you in your life, I'm here to tell you that you still have a voice—and your voice is needed. No matter what level of privilege the circumstances of our births have afforded us, it's time for all of us to wake up and own just how powerful we really are.

First, there is power in your mere *presence.* Just showing up can help heal the world. There is an annual celebration held every year in Austin to celebrate Martin Luther King Jr.'s birthday. *Every single year.* But it wasn't until I began meeting with a group of women, spearheaded by my African American friend Tasha, to talk safely and frankly about issues of race in our community that I knew I could attend. I thought that because I was white, I had no business marching in this event. I still viewed myself as part of the problem even though I have a black son; I disinvited myself from being part of the solution. The day that Tasha invited me to come along was the day I received the permission I sought. And as we marched that day, kids in tow, I realized how deeply my presence matters. And in case this comes as news to you, your presence matters too. If you've been waiting for official permission, then consider this your prompting to show up and *march.*

There is also power in your *voice.* I think about the time when Jalia went to the local Kampala police to speak up for her friend, Nakato, who was being abused. Jalia used her voice to empower another, and the result was a friend's life saved. Closer to home, after the recent horrifying race rallies in Charlottesville, Virginia, a Noonday ambassador commented to me that had it not been for her other ambassador friends using their voices to speak out, her Facebook newsfeed would have read like any other week during the time that the rallies occurred, containing no mention of them at all. But because our community has committed to living life awake and using our voices for good, she found herself surrounded by calls to action and messages of hope.

There is also a little something called *purchasing power*. Noonday's impact model is built on this power of purchases; every piece of jewelry sold creates and helps to maintain jobs in vulnerable communities. Personally, I love this model because it subdues my consumptive ways. I love to shop. I love to buy new clothes. And while I don't always buy fair trade, I do believe in voting with our dollars for the way of life we know is best. As long as Noonday prioritizes a long-haul view over cheap price tags and fast fashion, I get to join others in putting the humanity back into industry.

Additionally, after getting requests from artisan business partners asking for grants, emergency loans for health-care needs, and other needs that were still present in the lives of their artisans even with fair wages, we had to respond to our partners and friends. So, in 2015, we launched our corporate community-support program, the Flourishing World Initiative. Noonday customers use their purchasing power to create dignified work and fund adoptions; that alone changes the trajectory of lives. But when unpredictable emergencies and needs present themselves, our Flourishing World Initiative has helped fund things such as rebuilding homes of extended artisan families in Haiti after Hurricane Matthew, renovating roofing and electrical wiring of a workshop in Ecuador to ensure safe working conditions for their employees, and purchasing hundreds of water filters for artisan employees in Uganda.

On and on it goes. Our power activating their power . . . their power changing the world.

As you scan your life, do you see power flowing through you to others? Or do you see it lighting up in your life and the life of your family and then stopping abruptly there? If it has been a while since you intentionally channeled your energy, enthusiasm, skills, talents, and other resources toward someone in need, then I dare you to reverse direction and fuel another person today.

2. My Pocketbook: What if I became obsessed with generosity?

I know firsthand the power of generosity, because I have been on the receiving end of it throughout my life. My first job out of college was with Food for the Hungry, a role that required me to raise my own salary. For two years, I lived off other people's paychecks. My dad, a struggling entrepreneur for much of his early life, has always been a yes guy, whenever requests to help others come his way. Similarly, my mom never shied away from lending to someone in need.

By way of definition, generosity is the propensity to consider another's needs as more important than one's own and as such is a virtue of abundance. Not only have I been the beneficiary of generosity along the way, but truly, Noonday itself wouldn't exist were it not for the generosity of others through the years. Some of my early entreaties of God centered on finding an attorney who could help me craft an ambassador contract for our ever-expanding sales force. Knowing that I couldn't move forward without legitimate, legally binding paperwork, I reached out to some friends in lawyer-type circles and asked if they knew anyone who might be willing to help.

Soon after I sent that note, my friend Melissa replied. "Jessica," she said, "that's the type of law that my husband practices." An hour later, I was on the phone with Michael, Austin-based attorney extraordinaire, who agreed to help me—and pro bono, at that.

Several years later, Michael and Melissa invited Joe and me to an overnight event to be held in Austin, where we and eight other couples would talk about how to live more generous lives. We didn't know that those twenty-four hours would be spent on this subject, and neither Joe nor I knew most of the other couples scheduled to attend. But man, am I glad we went.

Our time was spent working through a book that Michael recommended, published by an organization called Generous Giving. We spent all of five minutes on niceties before diving into hard-core questions such as:

- How much money do I need? Will my answer always be "more"? Or can I set a finish line for myself and give away everything beyond that?
- If an outsider were to look at how I use my time, my energy, and my resources, what would she learn about my priorities?
- When money comes in, should giving rather than keeping be my default . . . not the exception, but the rule? Unless there's a compelling reason to keep, should I normally give?

Joe and I left that twenty-four-hour experience realizing that, because of the season of financial hardship during which we paid for groceries on credit cards and moved debt around like a game of chess, our approach to giving had become "How much do we give away?" instead of "How much do we keep?" Do you see the nuance? Instead of calculating how much money we had to give, we could instead plan a reasonable "keep" budget and then give the rest away. Acknowledging our fear and recalibrating our point of view toward one of abundance, instead of scarcity, created this shift in our giving and ultimately living. Because we believe that everything we own belongs to God, Joe and I wanted God to be in the role of CEO/owner/operator rather than financial counselor when it came to our stuff, our bank account, our vacations, our house, our everything. And so we began making changes accordingly.

Throughout years of international travel, I have come to expect certain questions abroad that would never be asked back home. Questions such as "How much do you weigh?" or "How much do you make?" or "Who did you vote for in your country's last election?" I'm telling you, the first time those were asked, I freaked. *Don't these people have a sense of propriety?* I wondered. *Isn't* anything *off-limits here?*

The truth indeed can be tough to speak, but I have to say, once Joe and I trusted those other eight couples with our truth regarding the delicate subject of finances, we were thrust out of our comfort zone into a space of greater freedom. Letting go of comfort *always* serves to free us up.

Remember sweet Tessa, adopted from Ethiopia by my friend Meagan? During our night away with those couples, I mentioned that Tessa's dad had just lost his job and couldn't draw on unemployment. Furthermore, since he and his family had recently moved into a wheelchair-accessible house, relocation to another city seemed an unthinkable option. The following day, I received texts from a few people in the group who asked if we could all pool our resources to cover what would have been the family's unemployment for four months' time.

I was blown away. The simple act of speaking truth about money had yielded a *ridiculous* amount of generosity. My friend, when we allow ourselves to be reminded that all we possess is sheer gift, generous living looks quite appealing; in fact, we would rather give than receive.

3. My Priorities: What if my schedule supported my "why"?

If we're going to set out on a path of lasting and meaningful impact, one thing is certain: we've gotta find the time. You can't give of yourself if there's none of yourself left to give, and you can't respond to the needs you see in the world that stir up your passion—what I call your "why"—if your schedule is already jam-packed. When I think about carving out space to serve others in my daily schedule, one of my favorite stories in the Bible springs to mind: the story of Boaz and Ruth. If you're not familiar with this Old Testament tale, let me give you the *Reader's Digest* version: God handed down a law to the Israelites commanding them not to harvest to the very edges of their fields. Instead, they were to leave the edges, the margins, unharvested so that the widows, orphans, and refugees could come gather what they needed. Boaz obeyed this law, and because he did he was able to provide economic opportunity for Ruth, a foreigner who had lost her husband.

This is the kind of room I want in my life—but I'll admit that I'm not there yet. You will catch me running from back-to-back meetings and saying yes to everything that comes my way. I am an opportunist with my time, which means that carving out margin is an ongoing challenge for me. But I'm determined to get better about "not harvesting to the edge of my field." I want to free myself so that I can give time and energy to others. I want to create space for addressing the needs I see.

Whenever I return from visiting one of our artisan partners in Guatemala, Peru, Haiti, Uganda, Vietnam, India, or any of the countries where we work, I am always reminded to *slow down, Jessica,* and to choose time with people over time with tasks. It's not that people in those places don't occasionally wish for more than a twenty-four-hour day; in fact, with no dishwashers, disposals, clean tap water, washing machines, microwaves, and drive-throughs, the actual living of life takes up a lot more space than it does in the resourced West. However, I can't help but notice that in those places, relationships seem to matter more than results. Which begs the question, Even though we may live worlds apart, could that not be the same for my life and yours?

On our recent family trip to Uganda, Holden and Jack spent the weekend with Jalia, Daniel, and their kids, while the rest of us visited the Nile River. I kept up with Jalia through WhatsApp, bantering back and forth throughout the day. But then came a serious note. "On our way to downtown Kampala, we found a man passed out on the side of the road," Jalia wrote. "Something told me to turn back . . ."

Jalia had suspected drugs as the culprit for the man's troubles, but in fact he was severely dehydrated. He had spent two days in the public hospital, where he'd received no water and no food—a common predicament for hospital patients who have no family in town to provide for their needs. And in Uganda, if loved ones don't bring you nourishment, you don't get nourished during your stay. The man had become so dehydrated that upon leaving the hospital, he passed out just one block away. He was unable to go on.

"Jessica, it's because we have a job and a car and money that we were able to help him," Jalia messaged me. "This is what Noonday has done for us." But what underscored that truth was that Jalia had let an inconvenience disrupt her schedule to live a people-first life. Now, *this* is how I want to live.

4. My Proximity: What if I proximated myself more to the problems?

What Jalia demonstrated that day was a willingness to come near to suffering and need. Bryan Stevenson, human rights attorney and author of the book *Just Mercy,* said it best when he told us to get proximate to the problems of injustice and inequality. "If you are willing to get closer to people who are suffering, you will find the power to change the world," Stevenson wrote, noting that he would not have wound up founding his incredible organization, the Equal Justice Initiative, had he not accepted a summer internship in law school that brought him face to face with inmates on death row.[3] His work during that season of life has saved the lives of more than one hundred wrongly accused death row inmates.

For Joe and me, this desire to *come close* is what caused us to rent our first apartment and eventually buy our first home in the less-resourced part of Austin. The desire to *come close* is what prompted us to enroll our kids in the public charter school they attend, where 40 percent of students are on free and low-cost lunch programs. The desire to *come close* is what compels us still today to befriend foster families, and to connect with diverse members of our community, and to shop at a grocery store that may not carry my favorite organic yogurt but certainly allows me to rub shoulders with people who are different from me. When that margin we carve out gets well tended, we find countless opportunities to come close. Still, I don't know what "coming close" will mean for you. I'm not telling you that you need to sell your house, uproot your family, and move to a needier part of town, but I am telling you that until you are comfortable at least *entertaining* the idea, you've got some bubble wrap yet to remove. What if the life you've been waiting for is waiting for you on the other side of town? Wouldn't you at least want to know that?

I began writing this chapter while intentionally holed up at a friend's house in Fort Collins, Colorado. As I drove around this quaint Front Range city, I noticed beautiful views, a mountain lifestyle, and predominantly middle- to upper-class living. "It's hard for people to find 'need' in this town," a local friend explained to me. "I mean, the average home price here is $380K." I wondered how I could exhort my reader to come close, if she lived in a town like this.

With that goal in mind, I drove around the following day. This time, I noticed a Habitat for Humanity ReStore building-supplies store, I saw a group of people who seemed to be shelterless sitting outside a discount grocery store, and I passed a trailer park on my way back home. I realized that, no matter where we live, there are invitations to come close, if only we open our eyes.

———————

There are other less obvious ways we can choose to come close too. For example, another way I have come close is by wearing jewelry pieces that were made by the people I've introduced you to in this book. When I wear a necklace forged in the fire of an Ethiopian village and later crafted together by my friend Addis, I proximate myself to her and to the son whom she is supporting via the sale of this beautiful piece. In this way, Noonday hostesses come close to people such as Mama Sham and others who are emerging from the vulnerability that poverty brings, simply by opening their front door and welcoming Noonday trunk show guests into their living rooms.

In a business setting, we can choose to come close by employing people who traditionally are considered less hirable than others. At Noonday, that has meant hiring several team members with refugee status, many for whom English is not their primary language. Truly, they are some of the most productive and most consistent team members in their departments. They have welcomed me and Noonday into their story of triumph and perseverance, an honor I wouldn't trade for the world.

When we choose to proximate with people who are different from us, we see need in a real and personal way. We develop relationships that enrich our own lives and give us the opportunity to connect with people we may never have encountered had we stayed wrapped in our bubbled cocoons. If we want to make a meaningful difference for others, it's imperative that we first *get to know them*. Standing off to the side, handing out water bottles and spare change, is not going to net the results we seek. To get the transformation we're after, we've got to get near, lean in, come close.

5. My Perspective: What if I relished rather than ran from paradox?

Prior to my midwifery stint in Bolivia, I attended a retreat in Austin, where author Richard Foster was speaking. Richard is a Quaker theologian and all-around genius when it comes to how spiritual formation occurs in a person. Bolivia felt like a huge move for me, and so before the conference ended, I responded to an invitation Richard made to the group to come to receive prayer from him. *Who in their right mind would refuse prayer from this guy?* I thought, as I headed for the front of the room.

When it was my turn to stand before Richard, I introduced myself, explained this move I was making, and thanked him for praying for me. He met my eyes, put his hands on my shoulders, and said, "Jessica, think of Mother Teresa. She received accolades before dignitaries in the White House one day and nursed ones who were sick and impoverished the next. My prayer for you is that you would never scorn the rich and that you would never glorify the poor. May you in peace just walk with them both. Be the bridge between them, Jessica, and walk in the spiritual path of peace."

As I sat with Richard's comments—especially that part about not scorning the rich—I recalled that I never would be heading to Bolivia with Food for the Hungry were it not for those debutante balls. At those parties, I looked into the eyes of scores of well-resourced people and, after explaining the mission I believed God had called me to, unabashedly asked them to fund my way.

Truthfully, I had also been guilty of glorifying the poor, the other half of Richard's caution to me. I'd refused makeup and new handbags all throughout high school, eschewing my mom's generous efforts toward me. I'd whittled down the stories of those living in poverty to fit inside nice, clean, compact bites: "They don't have any of our modern conveniences," I'd tell my friends, "but they're the *happiest* people I've met!" To make matters worse, I'd build atop this false narrative the errant exhortation to "live on less, and be happy, *just like them.*" What a load of crap. Poverty never makes a person smile.

Looking back, I can see that what Richard was saying was for me to *be Jessica*—whatever that meant. I didn't need to be Mother Teresa. I didn't need a habit and a homeless life. To walk alongside those God had placed in my path, I didn't need to flee the *me* God made me to be. I just needed the strength of my convictions, which centered on justice for everyone.

———

This paradox that Richard Foster exposed for me would be the first in a contradiction parade. Since the first days of Noonday's existence, I have worked to live in the natural tension that this type of life presents.

Appropriately honoring both the rich and the poor, engaging fully in both the world's suffering and its joy, appreciating both the progress and also the backtracks that are so common along this path—straddling so many opposing realities left me feeling like a cheerleader stuck in the splits. But an interesting thing happened the moment I quit trying to reconcile all of life: I started enjoying the ride.

I want to tell you that as you continue along on this journey, the *ands* only get more intense. It was one thing for me to realize that I could speak passionately about the plight of the poor while wearing both statement earrings and eyelash extensions; it was another thing altogether to find myself holding one of my Ugandan artisan's hands as she told me of the assault she'd endured, only to fly home the next day to my son Holden's biggest birthday-party concern—namely, how do we work the jets on our new swimming pool?

Paradox, anyone?

I have fielded urgent calls from our home office regarding artisans whose lives were in danger that very moment, even as I was scrolling through online sales, filling my digital cart with a new outfit.

From Ethiopia, I have FaceTimed with my kids to give them my digital version of a tuck in, after a day spent praying with women who nearly lost their children to poverty and prostitution.

I have taken a call from Jalia during a violent uproar due to the Ugandan elections, while walking around a hip, boutique hotel room I surprised Joe with for his birthday.

On the heels of these and a dozen other scenarios, I ask myself the same thing: "How do I respond well to the challenges my friends who live half a world away are facing, even as life here keeps on keeping on?"

I have to believe that as long as we allow ourselves to be burdened by such a question, we will be led to the answers we seek.

———————

During the time I was writing this, I had lunch with a new friend who was recounting her Noonday journey for me, and the more she talked, the more astounded I was regarding how well her story meshed with the considerations that you and I just worked through. Suzanne had won a trip to Austin through a recent Noonday campaign, and her story had my attention from minute one.

Suzanne and her husband, David, had adopted a child several years prior, after an agonizing, years-long wait. "People told us to quit trying to adopt," she told me, "that it obviously wasn't God's will for us, to which I thought, *Sometimes, people don't even know what to do with obstacles. I for one say, scale them.*" I thought I might grab Suzanne and kiss her cheek.

Despite those naysayers (and remember, you'll always find some naysayers along the path of imperfect courage), Suzanne and her husband made a commitment to growing their family through international adoption and then set about scaling every obstacle that got in their way. Suzanne didn't hesitate to put her time, energy, and money where her mouth was. She knew that if she was going to make this dream a reality, she would have to leverage every bit of power she had.

Finally, the family received some amazing news: they had been matched with a girl in South Africa who was waiting for them to bring her home. This was the news they had long waited for, and yet, if they had stopped when the first obstacle was before them, they wouldn't have been looking at their precious daughter's face in the photograph now before them.

In response to Suzanne's continued grit, one of her friends offered to throw her a baby shower by hosting a Noonday adoption trunk show.

For Suzanne, this trunk show represented a beautiful culmination of the passion for world change that had driven her this far and was a perfect way to celebrate her daughter. On top of that, the trunk show would help the family fund raise for some of those in-country adoption costs they were soon to face. Suzanne invited all her friends and many of her neighbors, most of whom she didn't even know, ordered a huge spread of African food, and was amazed at what followed. So many of her invited guests showed up to shop and listen to Suzanne and David's five-years-in-the-making adoption story. In the end, the couple ended up with a check from Noonday that almost exactly matched the cost of a plane ticket for their daughter's trip from South Africa. What?!

The journey toward adoption brought Suzanne right up against so many fears that could have easily stopped her in her tracks: Would she ever bring her daughter home? Would the slow gears of the international adoption system keep her in limbo forever? Was the long, long wait a sign that adoption wasn't in the stars for her, as some had suggested to her? But rather than letting these and so many other fears sideline her, she simply shrugged her shoulders and moved on.

"There are people all over this blessed planet of ours," Suzanne said to me, "who face far bigger fears than mine. They fear for their lives, they fear for their kids' lives, they fear disease, and they fear abuse. And yet what do they do every single day? They get up, and they get going." What Suzanne did and what we all can do is to match them step by fear-stricken step.

ELEVEN

QUIT TRYING

Someone is sitting in the shade
today because someone planted
a tree a long time ago.

Warren Buffett

WHEN AMELIE WAS SIX DAYS OLD, THE LACTATION consultant
called to see how things were going. "I just keep wishing I
could put her back inside me," I said, to which she replied, "Give the
baby to your mother and go to bed."

The woman was right; after five hours of sleep, I felt better, even as
the role of mother still loomed large. It was the inescapability of it all,
the *permanence* of it, that was freaking me out. For someone who thrives
on change, this was going to take some time to embrace.

Scaling a business has taken a similar toll. On the toughest days,
when I'm tempted to bail, I remind myself that I'm committed for the
long haul. My choice for courage has cornered me—and candidly, it
has been so good to be put in my place.

Similarly, to live a life of sustainable impact, you must take the long
view and think in more permanent terms. This means valuing a com-

mitment to long-term effort over short-term results and pausing as needed to take care of yourself so that you don't burn out before you've had the chance to see your vision through.

———————

When Jalia and I first went into partnership, there were no guarantees for either of us that we'd come out on the other side happy and whole. Who knew what would happen, really? *We* didn't—that's for sure. I think about those beginnings often—about how within eight months' time, the business had enough momentum for Jalia to employ seven artisans. I think about the one hundred artisans who work for her today, as well as the four hundred bead rollers in the broader community that she and Daniel have trained through the leaders in the organization they themselves raised up, and I just shake my head in wonder. *Wow. Look how far we've come.*

Throughout those first years, Jalia frequently had to remind herself that this wasn't a short-term deal. When you're living in poverty, she told me, if you had a meal for lunch, the tendency was to say, "Well, there won't be food for dinner," and this same fear-based, scarcity mentality naturally translated to our business arrangement. Even after we'd proven our concept, she was understandably nervous that soon it would all come to an end.

As Jalia and Daniel began to grow their business in partnership with Noonday, they were determined to make their workshop a place where families weren't just supported in their current state but rather were strengthened, made better, made whole. Most women in their community were single moms who had to make a difficult daily choice:

Would they leave their young children at home alone—vulnerable and unprotected—while they worked, or would they forfeit that necessary income so that they could stay home?

Jalia and Daniel had long dreamed of opening a day care center for their employees, and in the spring of 2015, that dream became reality. "My dreams are no longer about not leaving our kids as orphans," Jalia reminds me. "Because that dream has become a reality. Now I am dreaming bigger. I want to build my business so it will last for decades. I want to change the culture of my country so that women are respected and cherished. And I want to provide good jobs to all of Uganda!"

I could go on here and not just regarding Jalia's life change but regarding the transformation we *all* have known. But none of this progress unfolded overnight; great gains are made over great spans of time.

Along these lines, I often tell people to *quit trying*, a paradoxical-sounding piece of advice that I promise is more logical than it sounds. "I don't want you to *try*," I say. "I want you to *commit*."

Basic life experience assures us that this is true. How many times have I told myself, *I'm going to try to get to bed at a decent time tonight*, only to find myself still bingeing on *This Is Us* like it's my actual job when the clock strikes midnight? This choice of language matters, and it reveals the intention behind our words. For example, when you have a kid, you don't say, "I'm going to *try* to be there for my kid." No, you are *all in*, from minute one. You don't leave yourself an escape exit; you commit.

Now, I'm not saying that your goal of living a life of impact is the same thing as giving birth to a child, but it is a good comparison available to us. If you're going to really make this impact-rich, going-scared kind of life happen, you must commit for the long haul. I tell my Noonday team this all the time; long-term investment never shows profits in the super short term. And unless we all adopt a long-haul view of this partnership we're in, we will flounder around, trying this, trying that, never staying the course past what our naked eye sees. The generations-long perils that plague vulnerable communities, both at home and abroad, will not be solved in a finger snap. This work we're doing takes time and nuance; it takes patience and persistence and grit. And so my challenge to you and me both, and to anyone who says she longs for this impact-rich life, is this: *stay the course, fellow go-getter.* No matter what happens, stay the course.

- When cash is tied up in unsold inventory, what do I tell myself? *Stay the course.*
- When the company doesn't even come *close* to hitting the sales plan? *Girl, you gotta stay the course.*
- When the website crashes on Black Friday? *This is hard. But stay the course.*
- When a recently hired director of training resigns a month before our biggest event of the year? *Just keep staying the course.*

When we commit to staying the course, our eyes quit staring at the emergency exit in case things don't work out; rather, we go headlong into this risky and beautiful thing and say, "I believe in this so much that I'll go down, rather than threatening to bail, when things get tough." Commitment enables courage to corner us and makes apathetic comfort a nearly impossible option. As a result, we simply steer the plane through the inevitable turbulence across the ocean into the great horizon beyond.

And now I will be the first to tell you that our work in this world has barely even begun. So in the same breath as my telling you to take the long view here, I'm asking you to *pace yourself.* Indeed, a big part of staying the course is not running out of breath during the final mile.

———————

Not long ago, an ambassador named Rebecca told me she was "cutting back." She needed to pace herself in her Noonday business, she said, if she hoped to stay active not just now but for years to come.

Now, before I get to how I responded to Rebecca's update, I need to provide a little backstory on her. Soon after Rebecca and her husband were married, they expected to start their family, as so many of their recently married friends had done. But things weren't that easy for them, and that baby did not come. Not knowing what else to do, Rebecca dove headlong into her career as a successful paralegal and really made a name for herself. She was viewed by everyone in her field as the overachiever, the go-to, the most capable, most respected, most in-the-know paralegal around.

Eight years into their marriage, Rebecca and her husband decided to adopt a baby girl. And although Rebecca had been looking forward to motherhood for some time and was elated to be quitting her job, the transition from the workforce to the home front proved to be ridiculously challenging—mostly because nobody was standing there telling Rebecca how capable she was as a mom, or how respected, or how in-the-know. Her days were filled with dirty diapers, spit-up, and that certain numb restlessness that accompanies way too many nights logging way too little sleep.

"I joined Noonday to fuel that go-getter side of me," Rebecca said of that initial decision. "But because I was still attaching my worth to being perceived as strong, successful, and capable, I pushed too hard and let other things slide."

For her first three years as an ambassador, Rebecca's sales numbers bore out her unwavering commitment to Noonday, but by year four, life was way out of whack. "I didn't know exactly what was wrong," she admitted, "even as I knew something needed to change."

It took Rebecca a full year to sort out what kind of life she wanted and then to make the changes necessary to get from where she was to where she needed to be. And it was a stressful twelve months for her, untangling from that wrung-out and warped self-worth. She'd set the bar for self-care so abysmally low and the bar for Noonday success so sky high that trying to right her upside-down priorities felt like running a marathon on her hands.

By the end of that reprioritizing year, Rebecca had established some useful boundaries that would help her align what she said she wanted with the life she lived. For the first time in her life, she experienced a little thing called *balance*. "It was a hard-won and sometimes precarious balance," she admitted, "but it was balance, nonetheless."

When explaining her need to slow down to me, she looked me in the eye and said, "Jessica, what I've learned recently is that if I run hard and fast, if I put my pedal to the metal all the time, then I burn out way too quickly. I become no good to anyone."

"If I put my pedal to the metal . . ."

Those words were not lost on me. I had spoken those exact syllables to our ambassadors recently to fire them up to go for it. And although my role as a leader is to cast an aspirational vision for people to reach beyond themselves, only those individuals know how much gas is left in their tanks.

Rebecca continued, "I've learned that if I set my Noonday bar at a height that I can reach consistently, it means I can tend well to the rest of my life too. And that makes me a far better ambassador—not to mention a better wife, mom, neighbor, and friend."

———————

Perhaps you are wondering why, out of all the ambassador stories at my disposal, I am highlighting one from a person who is openly stepping back and pushing *less* in her Noonday business. What sort of salesperson am I? And on the surface, I admit, it seems a little counterintuitive. But the truth is, I don't want women like Rebecca to experience Noonday as a flash in the pan. I covet their partnership over the long haul; I want to work with them for decades to come. Which brings me to the response I offered upon Rebecca telling me she was cutting back.

"I am proud of you," I heard myself say to Rebecca, meaning every word. "You have cut loose from the jump rope of someone else's expectations of you, and you have found a pace for yourself that works. I hope everyone on our team chooses as wisely as you have chosen. You're really taking the long view here . . ."

The fact is that *consistency*—even if attached to a more measured pace—is what matters most to our artisan partners. Those hardworking entrepreneurs have told me on countless occasions that they would much rather have small but consistent orders than massive, infrequent jobs. "When we know that orders are coming, we can prepare for our production needs," one artisan recently told me. "Our entire group can now feel hope when thinking about the future." It turns out that when it comes to building dreams, slow and steady really does win the race.

———————

If anyone understands the tendency to go hair on fire in pursuit of a captivating vision, I confess to you that *I am that girl*. During the first

four years of Noonday, my life was *crazy* with a capital *C*. I was traveling way too much, sleeping way too little, couch surfing like it was my
profession, and eating less than healthfully, to say the least. I got strep
throat four times. I got shingles. I got insomnia, and I got fried. But
thankfully, my journey didn't stop there. Eventually, I also got wise.

I remember sitting on the couch with another bout of the flu,
googling things like "rest" and "boundaries." Maybe research *about*
self-care would mean that I was sort of practicing it? (My deep longing
for this osmosis style of actualization is evidenced by the unread titles
gathering dust on my bookshelf, all of which contain words such as
prayer, exercise, and *habits.*) In any case, I felt really committed this time
to applying what I would learn. I was tired of feeling tired.

I came across an article by Tim Keller, a pastor in New York, encouraging the keeping of a Sabbath. New Yorkers are known as hard
workers; I figured I could trust his advice on this.

Sabbath, which means "rest" in Hebrew, is a Judeo-Christian practice during which from sundown to sundown, one full day of the week,
you focus on enjoying God and resting from labor. Tucked inside
Keller's exhortation was a line so seemingly insignificant that I doubt
any other reader noticed it there. "Many . . . careers . . . demand some
sort of initial period of heavy, intense work. Starting your own business . . . will require something similar. In these situations, you have to
watch that you don't justify too little Sabbath by saying you're 'going
through a season'—when in actual fact that season never ends."[1]

For too many years as Noonday was getting her feet underneath
her, I hustled as a way of life. I looked forward to the minute when my
kids drifted off to sleep because *finally,* I could get some work done. If
my candle had had sixty ends, I would have burned them all; I believed
in Noonday's mission that much. And while I honestly wouldn't trade

those glory days for anything in the world, I recognize how unsustainable they were in the end.

Looking back, I see that during those early years I was not practicing wise pacing and I didn't even know what wise pacing was. Even after Noonday could afford to pay other people a salary, letting go and delegating was an entirely different story. I feel like writing an apology note right now to some of our first team members. So. Many. Midnight. Texts. "Did you remember to get that done?" I'd write. "Are you sure that everything's on track?"

And then, that team's all-time favorite: "Let's go in this new creative direction for the shoot that is *tomorrow.*"

This business was my fourth baby; could others be trusted to keep it alive?

In truth, it was time to look in the rearview mirror and put the pedal-to-the-metal start-up lifestyle behind me before it utterly ran me down. I needed to transition out of the sprint phase of the start-up and into the marathon phase of the growing company. If I've learned anything across the past seven years, it's that the twists, turns, and trials that we begrudge in the moment serve a significant purpose in the end.

In Guatemala, a weaver's most valuable possession is her backstrap loom, a portable weaving device that can be worn on the hips while the weaver goes about her daily life. Some of the most beautiful pieces I've seen have been weaved this way, and yet if you focus on the backside of the woven fabric, all you'll see is a tangled mess of zigzaggy colors, stray strings, and knots. It's when you turn it over that you see how those threads have come together to form a breathtaking design. And so it goes with our lives. You may think this season you're in will last an eternity—and when that season involves dirty diapers, do I ever feel your pain. I spent a few years of adulthood persistently damp either from using baby wipes to blow my nose or from using nursing pads to dam me up. That season is hard. And yet, it's still a season: it's here, and then it's gone. My start-up season needed to be gone now. My leadership needed to mature. And so, over time, I added back in monthly therapy appointments. I showed up at the gym again. I stashed my iPhone and laptop in an out-of-reach spot from 5:00 p.m. until the next morning. And the net effect of these important practices was that by pulling back in some places, I had more to give in the areas that mattered most.

These days, I know it's time for a little "me, myself, and I" intervention whenever I covet the job of the person who is foaming my latte. In the not-too-distant past, I happened to be feverishly working on a chapter for this book at a coffee shop around the corner from Noonday's offices, and for a good five minutes, I just stared at the coffee-making team. They were smiling. They were laughing with customers. They were seamlessly filling orders with lightning-fast speed. *Look how much fun they're having,* I thought. *Just think how life-giving that job would be.*

For a split second, I thought about submitting an application, which is when I came to my senses and realized that perhaps I was a teeny bit stressed. While gracefully serving others their caffeinated treats would be a rewarding pursuit, it doesn't serve Jalia. I shook my head as I slipped behind the wheel of my car heading home, muttering, "Tonight, the laptop stays *closed.*"

I don't know what the warning signs are for you, but my encouragement is to pay attention to them. This mission we've accepted to have global impact can feel heavy; we've got to know when to set the burden down. Toward that end, here are a few practices that I've found useful. Perhaps they'll serve you well too.

————————

First up: exercise. Between moving from Guatemala to Austin, getting married, and contracting mononucleosis—from Joe; thanks, honey!—I was hit with a bout of depression in my twenties that felt terminal to me. Still today, I have an article that I found during that season taped to a journal: "Depressed adults who exercised forty-five minutes a day did just as well as a group taking Zoloft." Then and there, I gave it a go, and I haven't stopped since.

I find that exercise has a halo effect on so many other areas of my life. I eat better, I feel more confident, and I have more energy. Plus, it's free! In short: *get moving, woman.* And thank me later.

Next, let's talk meditation. Now, you may think I have gone all "Austin" on you, but for real, it *works.*

For me, meditation is sitting with a truth about God for ten minutes' time so that the truth can spill over into my life. Over time, I've developed a simple set of phrases that I repeat to myself until I believe them to be true: "In your presence," I say aloud, "I have nothing to prove, nothing to change, and nothing to fix."

In your presence, I have nothing to prove. Nothing to change. And nothing to fix.

In your presence, I have nothing to prove.

Nothing to change.

And nothing to fix.

These words are my acknowledgment before God that I am worthy already, no bells and whistles added. I am here, I am present, and that is enough. I don't need to be thinner. I don't need to be smarter. I don't need every person in the Noonday sphere to enthusiastically support every decision I make. I don't need to convince all the school moms that it really is okay for me to travel for work. I don't need to do *anything more than what I'm doing* in that very moment. It is not a time of striving to *know* God as much as it is a time to experience what it is *to be known* by a God who always and forever has my back.

Being present, for me, is a challenge. I am the one during a workout class who runs over to my phone in the middle of a burpee to record a new idea in my notes, and I skip out on the last five minutes of stretching because, really, who has time for that? Being present takes work for me, and I find meditation wildly disruptive to my frantic ways. Still, I can't help but notice on those days when I begin with such centering thoughts that I breathe more deeply. I feel more rooted as a woman and as a friend. I view my life as an abundance of offerings instead of wrung-out, worn-out rags. I accept life as forward moving and eagerly jump into the flow. I am able to slow my hyperactive thoughts. I learn to be present, *right here.*

A third discipline I practice is connecting spiritually with my spouse. For years now, Joe and I have convened every Friday morning to pray together over our marriage, our parenting, our business endeavors, and our world. Joe is a man of few words, so what he speaks out in prayer gives me great insight into his heart. The unity that this practice has fostered, as well as the connection that it has brought, are worth the early morning wake-up call. Date nights are fun too, but this has brought depth.

I also value making time for friends. Travel can leave me feeling isolated, and so one of the strategies I employ before a trip is to set a friend date for when I return. The day after that three-week international trip that Joe, the kids, and I took, a couple of my friends dropped by with pizza and their herd of kids. Over pizza, piles of laundry, and suitcases not fully unpacked, I heard about their lives and their hopes for the coming school year while sharing some fun memories from our trip. They noted that the impromptu gathering would be the last thing they'd want after having been away for so long, but they knew exactly what I coveted upon walking back into home life, and they showed up eagerly to provide it. These are friends I wasn't close to even seven years ago, and as such, people in whom I would not have confided my needs. This is the reward of vulnerability.

Here's another discipline: There is the saying "It didn't really happen if I didn't post about it, right?" And yet, unfortunately, the saying is wrong. It is far easier for me to practice presence when my phone is not in my hands.

If you struggle to unplug from technology, then allow me to loan you a habit. A few years ago, I handed my children permission to unplug me if I didn't unplug myself. From the moment when I arrive home from work until the moment those beloved offspring drift off to sleep, Mama is to operate phone-free. And if Mama doesn't comply with this rule of hers, then one of them rats me out. So far, they've forgotten where they hid the phone only once. Admittedly, they do hide it with frequency.

Find practices that help you practically own your worth each day—regarding your body, regarding your family, regarding your work. Take responsibility for your one and only life so that you can empower others to do the same.

At last count, Noonday has established four thousand jobs in vulnerable communities around the world, which affect more than twenty thousand lives; we have launched more than four thousand ambassadors' businesses through the years, and we continue to employ fifty amazing staff at our home office in Austin. The stakes are high, a gut feeling I can quantify with cold hard facts. In the same way that Jalia can't just not show up one day and expect there to be no effect, none of us pulling for Noonday can in good conscience quit this work. And here I would ever so gently ask you: Do you see the high stakes of showing up for your life too?

I see great things in store for coming generations—absolutely, I do. I see an outright *revolution* spanning this globe of ours, and guess who is leading the charge? It's people like you and me, with a *contribution* to make. But those investments won't get invested well unless we seek to take a long-haul view. And so we pray. We recite truth. We schedule the therapy session. We book the massage. We buy the novel. We try on a little solitude for size. We do these things in order to care for ourselves. And, on occasion, for our sisters too.

In the last chapter, I told you about my friend Dee, who took in Rachel from Rwanda because she needed life-saving surgery at Dell Children's Medical Center of Central Texas. As I mentioned, Dee is a helper, while my role is to cheer her on. Don't get me wrong: I love to find systemic solutions for those in need; I'm just never going to love cleaning up vomit, which Dee says is the most honored task she does as a nurse.

When Dee and her husband, Tim, invited Rachel into their home and into their lives, they were hardly in a place for Dee to rest. I mean, there were now four kids to tend to, one of whom spoke no English and had significant medical needs. What was Dee supposed to do to stay sane, take the day off and go for a swim?

I knew that Dee was stressed to the max and that she would be in that season for quite some time. And while I couldn't necessarily remove that burden, I could put my shoulders right next to hers and bear

up under that weight. I did make it part of my regular rotation to leave
bags of groceries on her front porch, as well as to check in with Dee
several times weekly to see what she needed and when. I whispered her
family's names in my prayers, trusting God for their wisdom and
strength.

And then came an idea, one that a few friends and I saw all the way
through. Once Rachel's surgery was declared a success and Dee had
settled her into the school-year rhythm, those friends and I banded together to gift Dee with an *actual day off.* We arranged rides to school for
her four children. We gave her directions to a downtown hotel, where
two spa treatments were waiting for her. Later that afternoon, we met
Dee for a glass of wine, and we laughed and cried together. We made sure
her kids got home from school and started their homework, and we cared
for them so that she and Tim could go out to eat alone. In the grand
scheme of things, it wasn't much, what we did, but to Dee, *it changed
the game.* "I was refreshed at a level I didn't even know I needed refresh-
ment," she said, looking back. "That day was one of the best days ever."

This is peer pressure at its finest, my friend, which finds us celebrating long-haul ways. If you want to get going in life, then you'll need to
start trusting the one taking you there. It's just that it took me years to
find out who that *one* was. It turns out, the one isn't one at all—it's *us.*
We need each other in this journey, not just for now but for *all the days.*

A final thought, before we head for chapter 12: There are times when I
employ one of these spiritual rhythms—prayer or contemplation, solitude or rest—and I realize the reward of doing so right away. I feel
closer to the concept of peace, perhaps, or at least closer to the woman
I long to be. But just as often, I don't know immediate benefits. And in

those moments, I think it's critical to remember that the goal here is *effort* over any outcome that is achieved.

In the sales world in which I live, I understand that 80 percent of customers do not say yes to whatever it is you're asking them to do until you have asked them a *full five times.*

Yes, my friend, *five* times!

I share this statistic with the broader Noonday family all the time. "I know you want to give up after one or two asks," I tell them, "but human psychology just ain't on your side. Five times it takes, ladies—*five times.* You can take that one right to the bank."

Just as we need long-haul grit in sales, we need long-haul grit in choosing a life of impact. Frequently, I hop on Facebook Live with my ambassadors and say, "What are we celebrating today?" My team knows I'm not talking about results; I want some *effort* I can highlight and cheer. I want to know about the ambassador who made the fourth phone call (even though she was told no). I want to know about the teammate who gave herself grace to heal, following a wild bout with the flu (even though it meant she missed her own trunk show). I want to know about the rookie who led her first all-team phone call (even though she didn't know the answer to half the questions asked). I want to know about and celebrate effort, because effort over time is what yields lasting results.

––––––––––

Amelie's middle school hosted a back-to-school night earlier this fall, and as the principal explained the school's approach to education, my ears perked up. "We will be emphasizing a *growth mindset* in which learning is valued," the principal said, "rather than a *fixed mindset* in which grades reign supreme."

Yesss, I cheered silently, there from my seat. *My kid will catch this so much earlier in life than I did.*

Do you see it? You and I are going toward something, and we are growing as we go. We get the growth only by going, which absolutely is why we go scared. Fear enters the equation because we aren't experts. And yet something in us recognizes that to stay put is to stunt all growth.

If we hang our hat 100 percent on the outcomes we desire, you and I are probably going to be left wanting. We'll probably be disappointed and totally let down. That is the picture of a fixed mindset, of a fixed outlook, in which all eyes are on the prize.

But in a growth mindset, the prize is the journey. It's the process, the learning, the growth. A while back, my son Holden was teaching a buddy of his how to roller-skate. After a few clean misses and painful falls, the friend said to Holden, "Man, I am just so bad at this!" To which Holden said, "You can't be bad at something you've never tried before." I wanted to get that quote hand-lettered on my office wall.

When we commit, the issue of self-care becomes critical to our vision, and one that is squarely part of our growth. We grow as we go, and one of the main ways we grow is this: *How do I hustle and rest? How do I push and pray? How do I run and breathe?* We must learn to rest but not quit and to run hard while acknowledging life is all grace.

Only you will know the answers to these questions, because only you will know what you need. (Remember part 1 of this book? It was part 1 for a reason; learning to trust yourself is the critical first step.) My prayer is that you will learn to listen to your cues and respond to them with tenderness and grace. We can't get to where we want to go in life until we trust the us that is taking us there, and unless that us is healthy and hearty and whole, we won't arrive in one piece.

TWELVE

BUILD A FLOURISHING WORLD

Together we're building a flourishing
world where women are empowered,
children are cherished, people have
jobs, and we are connected.

Noonday Collection's vision statement

A s I STOOD OUTSIDE THE UGANDAN JEWELRY SHOP where it all
began almost seven years prior, twenty Noonday ambassadors
and dozens of artisans there at my side, the scene fell into slow mo-
tion as each face dancing around me represented yet another restored
life. As wild drumbeats rose from the percussionists' hands, I caught
sight of Bukenya, one of the most tenacious and loyal artisans in
the African Style group, not to mention the recently promoted production manager for the whole operation. *Weren't you the street kid
scraping by in Kampala?* I mused to myself, thinking back on things.
*Weren't you living in an orphanage, taking odd jobs to cover school
fees?*

At age sixteen, Bukenya was down but not out, struggling but determined to prevail. He'd aged out of the country's orphan program and thus had nowhere to go but the street. "I always knew I could be somebody," Bukenya told me once before. "So I took the first job I could find. I thought that I would finally be able to support myself."

That first job was laying brick for a local construction outfit. Except that Bukenya's bosses frequently "forgot" to pay him for his hard work. This was just how things went in Uganda, Bukenya said to himself. In this regard, he was hardly alone. In Uganda still today, a full 80 percent of adults aged twenty to twenty-four are unemployed, and those who *do* have jobs are rarely paid in full or on time.

Bukenya was living with his expectant fiancée, Coral, in the slums of Kampala, still doing odd jobs to try to make ends meet, when he met Jalia and Daniel, the very new owners of Noonday's artisan partner business nearby.

"We wanted to invest in this young couple," Jalia remembers, "so we helped them rent a one-room home. We paid their first month's rent, in exchange for them letting Daniel and me store a few jewelry supplies inside their home."

Neither couple knew at the time how prolific Bukenya was with his hands. Plus, he was a gifted problem solver, nimbly working out Noonday's most difficult designs. Because Bukenya was given an opportunity to change his circumstances, he trusted that life would look very different for that little baby Coral had been carrying. The cycle of poverty would end with her. With this hope in their hearts, Bukenya and Coral named their new daughter Shalom.

Shalom—*peace.*

Despite a life that had known only turmoil, Bukenya at last had located peace.

Peace that looked like a safe new home.

Peace that looked like a valued and profitable skill.

Peace that looked like viable work.

Peace that looked like a compelling future.

Bukenya and Coral were one of the nineteen couples that participated in the group wedding that December day in 2012, Bukenya the first of his father's children to officially, legally wed. From there, he went on to purchase land in town and is now saving to build his own home. Once, Bukenya saw himself as someone who would always struggle to survive. Now he has a job in which he can thrive and lean into his unique gifts. He has discovered his worth.

Behind Bukenya, I spotted Raeann, an ambassador from Seattle, shaking her booty and letting streams of tears flow. Raeann had recently been diagnosed with breast cancer and yet had fought tooth and nail to come to Uganda anyway. As I watched her soak in every second of this experience, I couldn't help but think about the other struggles she'd endured. Several miscarriages had left her still aching for a child. But she'd stayed the course with Noonday and used her voice to champion artisans and adopting families instead. She'd hit her stride, and she knew it. She had found her place and was more fully owning her worth. She had thrown everything she had into creating a marketplace for our partners across the globe, and now she was witnessing firsthand the fruits of all that work.

Latifa eased by me just then, her hips swinging a circle as wide as her broad, bold smile. This young woman had known so much trauma in her life, and yet look at those sparkling eyes now. If this girl wasn't the picture of flourishing, then I didn't know what was.

Latifa had come to Kampala from the village to find work when she was just sixteen. She sold used clothes, face creams, cosmetics—whatever she could find to sell. Unable to stabilize things for herself, she decided to move in with a man. "That's how I became pregnant with my son," she said, "when I myself was still a child."

By the time Latifa was twenty-one, she had two children, one of whom was chronically ill, and an abusive man on her hands. "The man treated me so badly," Latifa said, "that eventually I had to leave." Jalia told me that many people tried to get Latifa to give up her children along the way, but Latifa would remain steadfast: "I love my children. I will stay with them."

A mutual friend introduced Latifa to Jalia and Daniel, saying that she might be able to do housework for them. One thing led to another, and Latifa became an artisan for African Style. Now Latifa can afford rent for housing. Now she can afford medical care for her child. Now she can send her son and daughter to school. Now life is working well.

In addition to working as a jewelry maker, Latifa knew she wanted to start something of her own, to help supplement her income. As she considered what she should do, her thoughtful strategy impressed me. "I didn't want to sell bananas," Latifa explained, "because bananas, they can rot. But charcoal lasts a long time. I started with five sacks, and now I have ten."

Today, Latifa heads up the entire quality-control process for African Style, and according to Jalia, she is tough. "She never compromises quality, Jessica," Jalia told me. "If something is off, she'll send it back."

A few minutes after the welcome dancing subsided, Latifa pulled me aside to show me a picture on her phone of the land she had just purchased to build her mom a house. Although Latifa doesn't know a lot of English, her million-dollar smile said it all. We laughed together about how incredible it was that her life had changed so much—and not only her life, but the lives of everyone who knows her. Latifa knew that the best thing to do when you have more than you need is reach back and pull others up too.

I looked to my left and saw Heather, an ambassador from Austin, getting swept up into a series of irresistible hugs. Several years prior, there was no way that she could have imagined herself here, connecting with dozens of strangers half a world away from home. Back then, Heather was an introvert who didn't think she had what it took to speak in front of others at trunk shows. But I pushed her, seeing her far differently than she saw herself, and I'm glad that I did. Heather recently hit the quarter-million-dollar mark in lifetime sales and leads a thriving team of powerful women, each of whom has learned to own her own personality—and story—well. She had risked comfort in search of something bigger and better, and Uganda was delivering in spades. "This job has built up my confidence," Heather later said to me, "uncovered the lies I had bought into, and empowered me to leave my insecurities behind. You said yes a long time ago, Jessica, which led to my saying yes down the line."

Caleb was there too, a young man who had shown me his list, back when I'd met him on that first visit several years ago. "These are things I want to work toward," he announced, as he handed over a single tattered page. On it, I read of his hopes and dreams:

- mattress
- mosquito net
- plate
- fork

My own journey had begun with a list too, though mine looked quite different from his. "God, please, help!" I prayed. "Send me an

attorney. An angel investor. Send me some *help*." God had been faith-
ful to provide the right resources at the right time for each of us—a
valuable thing for me to see.

Rosetta approached as Caleb gave me a smile and a wave, and I
pulled her into a hug so tight that I think she believed she might just
burst. Her start had come when she went looking for work, going to
neighbors in her area to "see if they had a load." Rosetta was offering to
hand-wash laundry . . . anything for a few coins. "When they said no,"
she told me, "I asked about grass . . . Did they want any help planting
their compound?"

The day that she met Jalia and Daniel was the day that everything
changed. At last, she was able to support her four children. At last, she
could work, and *thrive.*

Seeing the pride that Rosetta had in being able to care for her family,
I thought back on how earlier in my entrepreneurial journey, I myself had
struggled to believe that I could be both a good mom and a good CEO.
Of course a person could be both! I didn't see Rosetta losing sleep over
being a working mom, did I? But for so long that was my everyday struggle. The sum of my life's work was creating profitable jobs for women who
are moms . . . and here I was, finally accepting my own offering.

As I surveyed the crowd that was bouncing and dancing outside of Jalia's
workshop, my eyes soon fell on Nakato, that shy and brave woman whom
I had first met seven years ago. She was the one for whom Jalia had stood
up, returning to the police station time and time again, demanding justice for the abuse Nakato had faced for years. "She is a different woman
today," Jalia tells me, "a woman totally and completely at peace."

That sociological phenomenon I have coined the Sisterhood Effect was birthed in this place, I am quite sure. I've seen it unfold too many times to count. As I moved through the crowd outside the workshop, I glanced over at Laura and Kelsie, two ambassadors who'd met at a Shine event three years prior, where they immediately became fast friends. Kelsie and her husband walked through a failed adoption recently, and to hear her explain it, she's not sure how she would have kept her head above water were it not for myriad late-night conversations with Laura, an adoptive mom. "It's the most beautiful picture of friendship," Kelsie said. "Laura's words literally healed my heart." And now here they were, together, celebrating what sisterhood had done.

Mama Jabal with her modest head covering also joined in the family reunion that was unfolding, and as I took in the delightful sight of her, I rejoiced in the progress she'd made. When I first met her, Mama Jabal was married to an abusive man, a man involved not only in witchcraft but also in multiple affairs. And because he was the only breadwinner, Mama Jabal and her two children had had no means for covering their own rent and food. Upon visiting her two years in, the first words she spoke to me were, "Jessica! I can leave my husband now."

Now, I don't make a point of facilitating divorce, but in this case, I was overjoyed. Her work, for her, meant *freedom*. It meant safety. It meant sustenance. It meant life. "I wish you well as you start this amazing new chapter," I said to her then, and that is exactly what she has done. Yes, her husband stole everything she owned on the day before she left for good. Yes, she had to rely on the goodwill of fellow artisans to restock her basic possessions. Yes, she had to exert incredible effort to build a new life for herself. But against such odds, *she did it*. She, and her family at the workshop.

───────────

At the sight of Mama Sham, I quit holding back my dammed-up tears. What a scare this woman gave all of us last year when she woke up paralyzed, and now look at her—*dancing*, no less. I met her bubbled-over exuberance with enthusiasm to match and then quite literally fell into her arms. As we embraced, Mama Sham pulled me outside the ring of dancers and whispered urgently, "Jessica! I have decided to follow Jesus. We are sisters now."

I loved witnessing the joy on her face in that moment, but the fact is, Mama Sham and I had always been sisters. "When we look across the globe, we don't see strangers—we see ourselves" is far more than a neat slogan to me. The truth of these artisans' lives is the truth for us all. As I basked in the joy of that impromptu dance party, I knew that back in 2010, when I drove over to San Antonio to pick up those donated crates of goods, my choice to go scared had yielded an outcome greater than I could have known.

As everyone settled in to eat the *matoke* with boiled chicken and greens that had been graciously prepared for us, Jalia stood up and tapped the mic. She motioned for me to come forward, and as I rose, I grabbed the hands of Joe, Jack, Holden, and Amelie, who had come too, and invited them to join me up front. Jalia asked me to share a few words with everyone, and as she handed me the mic, I took in my surroundings with humbled awe. It was hitting me little by little, just how amazing and unlikely this moment was. Here I was, a jump-first-look-later Texan with an education degree and a hodgepodge of a résumé, standing in front of more than one hundred people who had become extended family to me. We had walked through trials and joys together, celebrated one another's successes, and wept over one another's heartbreaks. None of us could have known whether this venture would take off, and yet here we all sat, proof that it had.

I looked beside me at Jack, the little boy who had started it all. I reflected on how unsure we were that he would ever be ours, on my hastily planned trip to DC to turn in our paperwork, and on my big stand in front of the judge that day in Rwanda. Jack was the reason that Noonday existed at all, and as I smiled at him, I wondered if he would ever truly understand how significant a role he had played. *All* of my family had played a big role. They had borne with me on so many occasions, through late nights and stress and haphazard attempts at dinner, sacrificing so much, to make this dream of ours a reality. And now here we all were, celebrating the progress that our fourth kid, Noonday, had made.

"This day feels like a gift to me," I told the crowd before me. "Seven years of partnership. The seventh year holds special significance in the Bible. It is when God told the Israelites to honor the Sabbath, to celebrate, to rest.[1] This is a celebration of completion, of coming so far. Remember when we thought we may not make it just two years ago? Well, we have. And I can't help but think about what the next seven years will bring."

As I finished speaking, I looked over at my friend Jalia, whose only dream when I met her was that she would survive so that her children wouldn't end up as orphans. Today her dreams are a bit bigger. "Jessica, now I am dreaming about a library and starting a marriage retreat center and how we can employ so many more people throughout the country!" she has told me more than once.

And I always respond, "Let's make that dream a reality."

Later, Jalia took our family to visit the farm that she and Daniel had slowly purchased, bit by bit, as is the custom in Uganda. They had already turned the farm into a sustainable food source for their employees, who now received a healthy lunch each day. As we walked, Jalia told me more about her dreams for the future. "We will have a chicken farm here," she explained as she pointed to the west, "that will help provide more food and income sources for our people. And we will have our marriage retreat center over there, where couples can come and learn what it means to have a healthy marriage, since so many people here have no role models to follow."

The last thing we did before we left the farm that day was to plant an avocado seed in the soil together. "We'll plant this today," Jalia said, wiping some dirt from her brow, "and in seven years, it will start to bear fruit." Then I will come visit, I told her, and we will make guacamole together. We laughed knowingly—Jalia's favorite Tex-Mex indulgence on her visits to Austin is chips and queso—always with a dollop of guacamole.

I loved this expression of Jalia's hopefulness, of her tenacity, of her long-view ways. Seven years ago, we had planted our businesses together and watered them carefully, hoping that one day they'd bear fruit. And against many odds, they had. Now, as we planned for the next seven years, I saw in Jalia this same future-facing orientation. The woman who had once lived one day at a time was now planting dreams that would blossom nearly a decade from now.

This hope was beautiful to behold, and it inspires me as I think about Travis's and my vision for the future. In this future, Noonday has multiplied in size but not lost the relational and personal qualities that make it so special. We have grown our ambassador community across the country and have invited thousands more hostesses to join us in building a flourishing world by opening their homes for trunk shows. We have impacted many times the number of artisans we initially dreamed of reaching, and we have worked hard to improve their lives holistically through work, education, life-skills training, and more. In this future, thousands more women have stood up, stepped into their stories, and owned their worth. And as we have linked arms together, agreeing to go scared, our en*courage*ment has only ignited more courage around the world.

———————

I'm often asked about how Noonday came to have its name. Since I was a kid, I've loved the verse in the Bible that says, "If you spend yourselves in behalf of the hungry and satisfy the needs of the oppressed, then your light will rise in the darkness, and your night will become like the noonday."[2] On a warm August afternoon, sitting on a boat dock soon after the night I had liquidated my inventory at the first trunk show, I dreamed about this little fund-raiser becoming an actual business. But if that was to happen, this business would need a name. It was then that those words from Isaiah came rushing back to me. I mulled over the verse a little longer before reaching for my phone, and when I did, I discovered an email from a friend I hadn't seen in some time. "I have been praying for you today for some reason . . . Just thought I'd reach out to see how you are." The note itself was relatively unsubstantial, until I reached the verse my friend had told me he had prayed for me:

If you spend yourselves in behalf of the hungry and satisfy the
needs of the oppressed, then your light will rise in the darkness,
and your night will become like the noonday.

That was my push, and so I jumped. I settled on Noonday then and
there.

·

———————————

Recently I was talking with my friend Wynne about what it means to
live life with an impact mindset. I met Wynne at the first event Noonday participated in, which was an adoption conference, back when Joe
and I were waiting on Jack. Wynne was wearing a cute headband, and
before even introducing myself, I asked if I could snap a photo of it, in
hopes that Jalia could whip up something similar that I could sell.
Wynne and I became fast friends, and within a few months, she joined
me as an early Noonday ambassador.

When Joe and I finally received the news that we were headed to
Rwanda to meet our son, I remembered that Wynne was a photographer. Would she be willing to come shoot our family's new "birth"
photos, I asked her, if we could find a way to fund her airfare?

Wynne later told me that she was honored that I'd invited her to
come and that, even more, this was just the start of my inviting her into
a more imperfectly courageous way of living. This revelation surprised
me—I was just doing the thing I always do, asking women to come join
me in whatever scheme I've dreamed up, but for Wynne it had meant
so much more. "I didn't realize that I was waiting to be invited into this
type of life until you invited me in and I said yes."

I eyed Wynne curiously.

"Jessica," she continued, "I'm representative of so many women out there. Women who don't think they're invited to come to this party, women who don't know that their presence is missed."

Instinctively, I knew what Wynne meant. I grew up in the handwritten-invitation era, when if you wanted to invite someone to a gathering, you stuffed envelopes with tangible cards. You then wrote the person's name and address and affixed a tongue-licked postage stamp. (If you arrived on the scene post-1980, then you're going to have to trust me on this; we once had to *lick* stamps, I swear.)

There was intention here, and thoughtfulness. Invitations required investments of care and time.

We have shifted into the Evite era now, and while I applaud the eco-friendly nature of this approach, not to mention the efficiency of it all, I think we've lost something important in the shift from then to now. Surely I'm not the only one who receives a digital invite and wonders, *Am I really invited to this, or did so-and-so just blast her entire database, hoping something with a pulse shows up?*

The sender could have labored over that guest list for hours, yet still I'm skeptical. *Hmmm, will she even notice if I don't RSVP?*

Reader, please lean in for a moment. Please picture my eyes, which are fixed on you. This invitation you've been waiting for? I have it, here in my hand. I'm handing it to you—can you feel it? Can you feel the textured card stock and its high-quality weight? And look there: your name has been hand-lettered, and I spelled it correctly—bonus points! I'm offering it to you, in hopes of your accepting it. I'm officially inviting you into this life.

What's more, I am standing right here until you reply to my invite. I'm immovable until then, fixed to this spot. Will you come? Will you show up? Will you risk a heartfelt *yes*?

Your presence is requested, my friend. Your specific presence—and all that that includes. We need you, exactly as you are, with your history, your struggle, your fear. We need your gifts, and we need your talents. We need your passions, and we need your pain. We need your personality, whatever it may be. We need your quirks and your not-so-perfect ways.

We need your college degree, or not.

Your love for reading to your children, or not.

Your love for international travel, or not.

Your love for artisanal jewelry, or not.

We need you, just as you are.

Where you are weak, another will bring strength.

Where you are strong, another will lean on you.

This invitation I'm handing you? It's to shine light like it's noonday, regardless of what the clock says. There is more to life than ease and comfort. You always suspected that this was so. My deepest prayer is that those things that kept you couch bound would no longer have sway over you and that today would be the day you stand up and choose a life of imperfect courage.

Come, my friend—come.

Come with your uncertainty.

Come with your questions.

Come with your anxieties and your fear.

This world is waiting for a beam of brightness, you see? A bit of noonday to light up the dark.

ACKNOWLEDGMENTS

I once took a personality test that nailed me. It said I thrive on a meeting of the minds. This tendency explains why, when it came time to write this book, I became excited only when I realized I didn't have to do it alone. My deep gratitude goes to Ashley Wiersma, Jenna Tanner, and Lindsay Hadlock. Your passion around this project matched my own. I believe our meeting of the minds made magic. This book is *ours*.

Noonday, and therefore this book, simply wouldn't exist without people who were willing to risk big on my behalf. I borrowed your belief more often than not in order to carry on. To Travis Wilson, my partner in crime: I am a better leader because of you. To Suzanne Wilson, who saw the potential impact that Noonday could have long before the rest of us: Thank you for your grounding wisdom.

Thanks to Laura Morton, for inviting me to visit you in Uganda and for playing such a significant role in the unfolding of this vision. Thanks to Downie and Bobby Mickler who created an opportunity for me because you saw a future for Jalia and Daniel Matovu.

Thanks to Jalia and Daniel Matovu, whose love for the most broken and vulnerable teaches me daily. You opened the doors for thousands of artisans around the world. I am forever grateful to all of our artisan partners—who dealt with purchase orders done in email paragraphs, and who have always been willing to try new designs and innovations. Your love for your people has given me a deep love for your people. This is your story.

Thanks goes to Sara Brinton who created a path for thousands of ambassadors to follow. To those women who said yes that first year to the ambassador opportunity when our only real skill was scrappiness: You formed a foundational culture that is changing how women are perceived around the world. Thank you to Allison Humphries, Beth Bernhardt, Brittany Gaskill, Courtney Garrett, Elizabeth Chambers, Katie Fickey, KK MCKenzie, Krista Box, Lindseay Schmierer, Lisa Foster, Liz Bradley, Lori Boynton, Mary Barker, Rebecca Williams, Renee Dubose, Whitney Ray, and Wynne Elder. And thank you to those who have been building this community with me for six years now: Krista Box, Lisa Foster, Brandi Mendenhall, Holly Wimer, Paige Knudsen, Kate Halaris, Jen Thrift, Susan Hood, Melonie Rosenfarb, and Carrie Glanzer.

To my world changing active ambassadors, whose continued belief in me has unlocked a courage I didn't know was there, thank you. Many of you told me to write a book some day. Thank you for speaking that out loud. This truly is for you.

To those who loved on my kids when Noonday was in triple digit growth: Lauren Bazan, we are changed because of you. You infused so much peace into our home during a chaotic season. And to Lyndsey Sweeney, thank you.

It's a real challenge to learn on the job when that learning curve impacts the people you are leading. For Joel Skotak, Renee McCharen, Johanna Robinson, Jaclyn Dowdle, Nicole Schuman, and Shelly Smith, those early team members who joined us when we were building the plane as it was flying, *thank you*. Thank you to Karen Gibbs who blazed this trail long before anyone knew what artisan goods were. Thanks to Arturo Coto who has epitomized adaptability and faithfulness and who has taught me so much about leading people. To my current teammates at Noonday: You guys *rock*. Thank you for picking up the slack for me during this entire book writing process and for adapting to my schedule even when it was not convenient. Thank you to the rest of the executive team, including Sheila Walker and Christy Kranik, for carrying this vision with us.

Behind anyone who has known even a speck of success is an army who has her back. To my loosely formed collective of women who get the calls and SOS texts whenever I'm tempted to throw in leadership's towel: Jennie Allen, Jen Hatmaker, Melissa Russell (extra props for helping with the early version of this book), Mica May, and Jamie Ivey, thank you for *always* answering my calls. To Sara Combs, Meagan Brown, Lori Newell, Stacie Chilton, and Dee Brosnan, the friends who love me so tangibly it's as if God makes himself incarnate through you; I know for sure you will move in to my house if tragedy strikes, and you know I have you covered on the best memorial photos ever.

Thank you to those who read the early manuscript. Jesse Cougle, Marijoy Horton, Christy Kranik, Romy Parzick, Suzanne Wilson, Melissa Russell, Joe Honegger, and Travis Wilson provided invaluable feedback. And thanks, Tim Willard, for your help on chapter 3. Thanks to Shauna Niequist for connecting me to Chris Ferebee and Ashley Wiersma and for being an energetic cheerleader for the book.

And thanks to the stellar team at Penguin Random House. To my agent, Chris Ferebee, and to my acquiring editor, Shannon, thank you for walking with me through this process. Firsts are never easy, but you made my hesitant steps more walkable. Thanks to each of you at WaterBrook and Crown for collaborating on this project, and to Tina Constable for believing in the original proposal.

To my children, who see the best in me and who remind me to put down my phone and opt for dance parties, games, and the Hallmark channel instead. I can't wait to see all the ways that God will guide your path. Amelie, thanks for never letting me text and drive and for walking in deep friendship with me. Holden, your shoulder rubs always bring comfort, and your positivity brings sunshine into our home. Jack, your bedtime cuddles are the highlight of my day, and your unearned trust has forever changed me. You changed my whole life. I will never grow tired of your asking me to massage you, so I hope you keep asking. To Joe, your roots go down so deep. Your shade covers us, refreshes us, and gives us everything we need to step out into the harsh sun to keep living courageous lives. We belong to each other, and that belonging has brought a deep sense of security. You make me brave.

To my parents, who saw my fire and let it burn: Thank you for fostering my independence and loving me fiercely, even as you let me venture into the world at such a young age. To my brother, who, though we are each other's opposite and walk to the beat of our own drummers, I have always loved your drumbeat.

Thank you to my mother- and father-in-law who have supported me and our family every step on this journey. Your sacrifices to help out with the kids, your steady love and support, and your deep love for those in needs have steadied me.

To those who wrote words long before me that impacted my views, shaped my leadership and eased some of the loneliness that comes with braving new paths, your work matters to me and helped give me the courage to write this book: Andy Crouch, Dr. Brené Brown, Dr. Curt Thompson, Darrow Miller, Gary Haugen, Sheryl Sandberg, Shonda Rhimes, Tim Keller, Tina Fey, and many others. I'm grateful for you all.

To my Jesus: You caught my attention at a young age and fostered a love for the vulnerable that could only have been orchestrated by you. Thank you for the opportunities you continue to afford, which in turn spark opportunities for others. Because of you, I feel known, loved, accepted, and brave. May all that I say and do in this life be a love song to you.

NOTES

Introduction: Give It a Go
  1. This pier is featured in the photo on the book's cover.

Chapter 1: Choose Courage
  1. Andy Crouch, *Strong and Weak: Embracing a Life of Love, Risk and True Flourishing* (Downers Grove, IL: InterVarsity, 2016), 76.
  2. Crouch, *Strong and Weak,* 89–90.

Chapter 2: Stand Up
  1. Joe Hadfield, "Study: Deciding by Consensus Can Compensate for Group Gender Imbalances," *BYU News,* September 17, 2012, https://news.byu.edu/news/study-why-women-speak-less-when -theyre-outnumbered.

Chapter 3: Step into Your Story
  1. See http://pottershousedc.org/history.
  2. Sheryl Sandberg, *Lean In: For Graduates* (New York: Knopf, 2014), 170.
  3. Brené Brown, *The Gifts of Imperfection: Let Go of Who You Think You're Supposed to Be and Embrace Who You Are* (Center City, MN: Hazelden, 2010), 57.
  4. Alen Standish, "The Perfectionist and Perfectionism," *Quit Binge Eating,* July 3, 2014, www.quitbingeeating.com/pnp041-the -perfectionist.

Chapter 4: Own Your Worth

1. Tina Fey, *Bossypants* (New York: Little Stranger, 2011), 23.
2. Geoff Williams, "The Heavy Price of Losing Weight," *U.S. News & World Report,* January 2, 2013, https://money.usnews.com /money/personal-finance/articles/2013/01/02/the-heavy-price -of-losing-weight.
3. C. S. Lewis, *The Weight of Glory and Other Addresses* (New York: HarperOne, 1980), 109.
4. Genesis 1:31.
5. Brené Brown, "Finding Our Way to True Belonging," Ideas.Ted .Com, September 11, 2017, https://ideas.ted.com/finding-our-way -to-true-belonging.
6. Karyn Purvis, *The Connected Child: Bring Hope and Healing to Your Adoptive Family* (New York: McGraw-Hill, 2007), 19.
7. Kyle Benson, "The Magic Relationship Ratio, According to Science," The Gottman Institute, October 4, 2017, www .gottman.com/blog/the-magic-relationship-ratio-according -science.
8. For more information, please visit "Person-Centered Language," Mental Health America, http://mentalhealthamerica.net /person-centered-language.

Chapter 5: Embrace Vulnerability

1. "*The Oprah Winfrey Show* Finale," Oprah.com, May 25, 2011, www.oprah.com/oprahshow/the-oprah-winfrey-show-finale_1 /all#ixzz56WbGC9ul.

Chapter 6: Create Compassionate Spaces

1. See Jeremiah 29:11.

Chapter 9: Widen Your Circle

1. Thomas R. Eisenmann, "Entrepreneurship: A Working Definition," *Harvard Business Review,* January 10, 2013, https://hbr.org/2013/01/what-is-entrepreneurship.
2. Christina Breitbeil, "Ben and Jerry's Co-Founder Emphasizes the Ethics of Business," *The Daily Texan,* January 5, 2014, www.dailytexanonline.com/news/2013/11/20/ben-and-jerry's-co-founder-emphasizes-the-ethics-of-business.
3. Jim Clifton, "What the Whole World Wants," *Gallup News,* December 17, 2015, http://news.gallup.com/opinion/chairman/187676/whole-world-wants.aspx.

Chapter 10: Leverage Your Power

1. Gary Haugen, "God's Plan for Justice," *Christianity Today,* June 1, 2009, www.christianitytoday.com/pastors/2009/june-online-only/godplanjustice.html.
2. "Conscious Capitalism Credo," Conscious Capitalism, https://consciouscapitalism.org/about/credo.
3. Ellen McGirt, "Overcoming Trump Anxiety: Lessons from a Civil Rights Leader," *Fortune,* November 15, 2016, http://fortune.com/2016/11/15/bryan-stevenson-justice-hopelessness.

Chapter 11: Quit Trying

1. Tim Keller, "Wisdom and Sabbath Rest," Q Ideas, October 2014, http://qideas.org/articles/wisdom-and-sabbath-rest.

Chapter 12: Build a Flourishing World

1. See Leviticus 25:4.
2. Isaiah 58:10.

BETTER TOGETHER

At Noonday Collection, we have a big vision: to build a
flourishing world where women are empowered, children
are cherished, people have jobs, and we are all connected.

Want to join us in making a global impact?
Visit noondaycollection.com to learn how you can join our
community as a Noonday Ambassador or Trunk Show Hostess.

noonday collection®